Praise for *Walking on Pins and Needles*

"I have known Arlene since I started my integrative medicine and neurology practice at the Heartwood Center in 2013. I know firsthand the healing effects of Arlene's Tai Chi classes through the experiences of our mutual patients and clients. After reading her memoir, I am honored to know such a truly exceptional individual. Her book documents her journey as she navigates the highs and the lows of life with multiple sclerosis. More importantly, it's an inspirational account of the power of self-healing. I highly recommend this book to anyone going through their own personal health and healing journey."

—**Rowena Chua**, MD, Integrative Medicine and Neurology

"In *Walking on Pins and Needles*, Arlene Faulk delivers a gripping memoir of her exciting professional trajectory, first interrupted, then ultimately flattened, by chronic neurological disease. Hitting a dead end with western medicine, she explores other healing modalities, including the ancient, low-impact movements of Tai Chi. Slowly, steadily, her health returns. A powerfully inspirational story, exquisitely written."

—**Christopher C. Cinnamon**, JD, MS, head instructor, Chicago Tai Chi; author of *Tai Chi for Knee Health: The Low-Impact Exercise System for Eliminating Knee Pain*

"This is an amazing story of resilience. Arlene finds a way to reinvent herself, obstacle after obstacle. Along the way she finds the healing powers of Tai Chi, and as typical for her, uses this to help heal others. This book is a living example of the impact exercise and a positive attitude have on health. It is also a reminder for those of us in the medical field to be persistent in finding positive solutions for our patients and acting as their partners in health. An excellent book to read and share with others who need inspiration!"

—Lisa Kokontis, MD, neurologist

"With a quiescent calm and intimacy, Arlene takes us on her journey from getting off the couch to teaching Tai Chi in response to a debilitating disease. When western medicine offered no or unsatisfying answers to what she later learned to be multiple sclerosis (MS), Arlene listens to her body and embarks on the world of eastern medicine and changes her life. This is an inspiring read for acupuncture and Tai chi students & practitioners and for those with chronic illness who are bold enough to look outside of the box."

—Dr. Lori Howell, L.Ac., DAOM, associate professor, Pacific College of Health & Science

"This riveting book tells the astonishing true story of Arlene Faulk's reshaping of her life as she reclaimed it from multiple sclerosis. From her start as one of few women climbing the corporate ladder, she movingly takes us, step by step (literally), through her wrenching descent into a nearly immobile existence—and then her miraculous rise into an active, happy life grounded in the practice and teachings of Tai Chi. Like its author, the book conveys deep truths with deceptive simplicity, straight from the heart. Along with her many other students, I've found inspiration and healing in Arlene's approach to teaching Tai Chi, a gentle way of re-orienting those of us with physical challenges whose echoes resound through this compelling narrative."

—Elizabeth Mertz, JD, PhD, long-term Tai Chi student

"Arlene Faulk's memoir of self-healing shows two decades of ignoring symptoms, burying suffering, and refusing to quit. Her succinct, unadorned chapters read like eating popcorn. No woo-woo, no religious visions, but powerful, simple 'steps' that change her illness to life energy."

—Nancy Beckett, founder of Beckett & Company,
Creative Writers' Collective Chicago

"Arlene vividly shows how perseverance, changes in lifestyle, and daily commitment to healthy exercises can lead to health. She lives out what I've learned through my years of clinical research. Be inspired and get ready to begin your healing journey, a step at a time!"

—Terry Wahls, MD, author of *The Wahls Protocol:
A Radical New Way to Treat All Chronic Autoimmune Conditions*,
and clinical professor of medicine at the University of Iowa

WALKING

ON PINS

and

NEEDLES

A Memoir of Chronic Resilience in
the Face of Multiple Sclerosis

ARLENE K. FAULK

RIVER GROVE
BOOKS

Some names and identifying characteristics of persons referenced in this book have been changed to protect their privacy.

Published by River Grove Books
Austin, TX
www.rivergrovebooks.com

Distributed by River Grove Books

Design and composition by Greenleaf Book Group and Mimi Bark
Cover design by Greenleaf Book Group and Mimi Bark
Cover images used under license from ©Shutterstock.com/nicostock; ©Shutterstock.com/Anne Mathiasz; ©Shutterstock.com/Annartlab

Publisher's Cataloging-in-Publication data is available.

Print ISBN: 978-1-63299-492-9

eBook ISBN: 978-1-63299-493-6

First Edition

For Mom and Dad

"When I let go of what I am, I become what I might be."

—LAO TZU, Chinese Taoist philosopher, b. 600 BC

Contents

Contents

Prologue

I am twenty-two years old on the afternoon when all feeling in my body vanishes from my waist down. As a management trainee alone in the stockroom of my department store, I extend my hand to touch my leg. Nothing. After kicking off my left shoe, I rub the sole of my foot across the floor. Nothing. My brain urges my foot to take a step. As the weight of my leg hits the floor, my knee buckles. It's the day after Thanksgiving, the busiest shopping day of the year. All hands need to be on deck. This is the day I have to show leadership, rally the team together to handle the multitude of shoppers.

My head spins. *What's going on? Am I going to be paralyzed?* My heart pounds, faster. And faster.

This wasn't part of the plan for my life. Just a few years before, I'd been voted "Most likely to succeed" as a senior in high school. I am on track to live out that label. Growing up in a town of 7,300 people in northern Illinois didn't stop me from dreaming big. At thirteen, I saw myself as a professional basketball player. At sixteen, I thought I might be a female Roger Ebert, an A-list movie critic. I grew up believing I could do anything, be anything, through hard work and with an education. I saw Mom and Dad exhibit qualities of perseverance, working long hours, saving money. My brother, sister, and I all had a bank account by the time we were six years old. We weren't rich, but Dad, a family physician who emigrated from Europe, developed a thriving practice from scratch.

I kept the strong work ethic I inherited from Dad and Mom when I went off to college in 1966. Diligent with my studies, I faced social upheavals outside of class. During my sophomore year, parties with beer and scotch changed to marijuana and quaaludes. Student anger increased toward the Vietnam War, with regular protests and violence on campus. I, like many fellow students, lost trust in government leaders. They lied. I lost trust in big companies like Dow Chemical. Its Agent Orange killed people. As a journalism major reporting for the University of Iowa newspaper, I interviewed people and researched events that gave me an up close and personal account of how those in power made decisions, how many of their actions were self-serving, contributing only to their wealth and power.

As my senior year progressed, my direction after college wasn't clear. Maybe I could strive to be a leader, with enough authority to make decisions that could positively impact a broad range of people, not just a few. While in college, I was elected to a university-wide judiciary committee and got a lot of ridiculous rules for women, like curfew, thrown out. During year three when I chaired the committee, we got the entire judiciary process abolished. When I accepted a management trainee position at this department store right after college, I hoped to continue my work to change outdated policies from the inside.

Now on a November afternoon in 1970, three months into my new position, my body caves in. My world caves in. Having enjoyed great strength for all my years to date, I'm stunned, petri-fied, fearing my big dreams will not become reality. As I get up to take a step and falter, I quickly return to the chair in the back corner of the stockroom. I'm not sure if I can get up and walk a few steps without falling.

A heavy fear consumes me. What is happening to my body, and will I ever walk again?

— CHAPTER 1 —

The Biggest Shopping Day of the Year

Three months earlier I'd moved to Minneapolis, to my first apartment on a tree-lined street four blocks from the Minneapolis Institute of Arts. I was so pumped to start my job as a management trainee for Dayton's, a national leader in the retail department store business.

From day one, it was like sprinting out of the starting gate at the Kentucky Derby. I and my seven fellow trainees, eager to learn and prove ourselves, displayed our youth and vigor as we jumped into all assignments thrown at us. My department was fine coats. From the first moment I entered the sales floor, it was bustling with customers trying on coats of all kinds—wool, leather, cashmere—and most walking out with a purchase.

Twelve-hour days became the norm, starting with a staff meeting a half hour before the store opened. I spent a lot of time on the sales floor talking to customers, seeing the traffic flow patterns firsthand, and learning how seasoned sales staff marketed and sold. My boss, John, and I reviewed each day's sales in comparison to projections. I rarely got time to sit down for lunch and was not bothered by running around all day in my two-and-a-half-inch heels. Downtime didn't exist.

The fast pace suited me. In college, what I had enjoyed most as a journalism student was reporting for *The Daily Iowan* university newspaper. I'd loved the rush, capturing the story on-site, zooming into the newsroom, hearing the clickety-click of multiple typewriters, handing off my story to the editor and hearing, "Run it with byline." Music to my ears.

This department store management trainee position provided similar momentum, focused on results and high goals to shoot for, every day a new challenge. Most staff had been helpful in sharing their years of experience and sales expertise. The fast pace and intensity were even higher as we prepared for the day after Thanksgiving, the busiest shopping day of the year.

On that Friday, I was at the store at 7:00 a.m. Shoppers lined up outside the doors an hour before the store opened. When the buzzer sounded, the doors flew open, and a sea of shoppers flooded our sales floor on a mission to buy.

After five hours with no restroom break, my body was calling for relief. As I dashed to the far end of the sales room, a sharp needlelike pain pierced my right ankle. Electricity flowed from my ankle up my leg. Standing so long could take a toll even on a twenty-two-year-old. But I had to keep moving. Around 2:00 p.m., feeling light-headed, I walked down the hallway to the employee cafeteria. I picked up my bowl of soup and took it to a small table. As I sat down, I realized there was no feeling in my right hip. Numb. What was happening?

2

What was I to do? Eating didn't make me feel better and getting up on my feet made my body feel weak and shaky. Slowly, as I walked back to my department, the feeling returned.

It was a madhouse around the coats department, so many people racing around, coming and going. It was enough to make anybody's head swirl. My focus was on the dance in my body, alternating from needlelike pain to numbness. As I made my way back to the stockroom where it was quieter, my eyes zeroed in on the single chair in the corner.

My brain was in a fog. Who knows how long I was sitting there before my head clicked in to tell me I had lost all feeling from my waist down to the soles of my feet.

– CHAPTER 2 –

Tests

A muffled voice interrupts my stupor. The voice gets louder. "Are you okay, Arlene? Are you okay?" My gaze turns to the left, where my boss is crouched down in the stockroom, talking to me. "Are you okay?"

"No, I'm not okay," I respond. "My body has gone crazy and I've lost all feeling from my waist down. I'm scared."

The next thing I know, we're sitting in a doctor's office waiting room. My boss has pulled some strings to get me in to see his family physician. We wait only twenty minutes until he sees me. Normal vital signs. Symptoms seem to be neurological, he suggests, and I need tests. *Tests? What kind of tests? And what about walking first?* I feel alone here, new to the area. I need to call Mom and Dad.

Out of the doctor's office, my boss accompanies me safely into my apartment. My hands grip the back of my sofa to steady my balance. I'm about to call Mom and Dad when the phone rings. My brother-in-law excitedly blurts out, "You're an aunt for the second time! Mom and baby girl, Stacy, are doing fine."

"What great news, a baby girl," I say, hoping my voice sounds upbeat, not shaky and weak. I'm hurting, frightened, yet I say nothing about my situation, not wanting to spoil their exciting news. My spirit sinks as I put the receiver back on the phone base. My heart longs for family support right now, but they don't need their spirits dampened, too. I'll call Mom and Dad in the morning.

After a restless night of tossing and turning, I brew my cup of coffee, getting ready for my phone call. My beige rotary phone sits on the table. *How do I say it? Do I just blurt it out?* I rub my fingers back and forth on my chin. Mom will stay calm, but she'll worry and have trouble sleeping. Dad will become overprotective and want me to move closer to home. He'll fixate on getting me in to see the best doctors, to Mayo Clinic, if needed. He'll fret, which will make Mom worry more.

I stand up. Still no feeling. My hand approaches the receiver as I sit back down.

"Hi, Mom. I have something to tell you. I'm not sick but had a weird thing occur yesterday." I spill out what happened. She quickly gets Dad to join us on the phone. He wants to get me into the University of Iowa Hospital for tests. Even though it's a holiday weekend, Dad works wonders and sets up an appointment for next Wednesday. Mom will drive to Minneapolis to pick me up, then go directly to Iowa City. Dad will meet us there. He has so many sick patients to see on Monday that he can't take the day off.

It's no surprise he can't come with Mom to pick me up. He has always been totally dedicated to his patients. I remember, as early as five years old, being excited about a two-day trip to Wisconsin Dells. Imprinted in my head is how hard it was to get our family out the door and into the car. Getting *Dad* into the car, I should say. My older brother and sister, David and Carol, were already in the car. Dad was in the house talking on the phone, probably to the hospital staff, about one of his patients. Mom stepped into the garage with the picnic basket of our favorite sandwiches, cookies, and brownies, the last thing to pack. She made sure the Hi-Q board and tic-tac-toe paper sheets were in the back seat.

We were ready to go. No Dad. Mom suddenly disappeared into the house, the screen door slamming behind her. I couldn't make out much of what Mom and Dad were saying, but I did hear Mom say, "Come on, Elliott. Let's go. Your patients will get along without you for a couple days."

Now, because of my health scare, Dad takes Wednesday and Thursday off to get me the best possible care, and meets Mom and me in Iowa City. On Wednesday morning, Dad, Mom, and I sit in green, straight-backed chairs in a neurologist's office at the University of Iowa Hospital complex. Each of us, magazine in hand, try to pass the time, which seems to be moving in slow motion. *How serious will this be? Will the tests hurt? Will they have lasting effects?* My career plan does not include spending time undergoing lots of medical tests.

"Miss Faulk?" the medical assistant calls out, by a door to my left. I grab Mom's arm on one side and Dad's on my other side and we walk slowly into the doctor's office.

When we enter the room, Dad takes charge. He explains why we're here. Then the neurologist peers over his half-glasses and asks me to recall the events leading up to the loss of feeling. He also wants to know about my health issues as a child, as a teenager. I respond that my health until now has been excellent.

As I sit on an examining table, he has me reach out my hand, move my index finger to my nose, then out in front, and back to my nose again. He takes a little silver flashlight, with an intense beam, and shines it into my eyes. Next, he asks me to look peripherally to my right and tell him how many fingers he's showing me.

"Here's what I think we need to do," he says, looking directly at Dad.

He tells Dad, with Mom and me listening, that he wants me to have a CT scan and a spinal tap with an additional procedure to inject air into the spinal column and then take X-rays.

"Arlene will have to be hospitalized for two days," he says. "We can admit her tomorrow," he adds, talking about me in third person, like I'm not there. *Am I invisible? Hello, Doctor, I'm here. Look at me.* Dad is a physician, but I'm the one who has to endure everything. I want to matter.

During the next two days, I go through the tests. Mom and Dad sit in my hospital room, waiting, only leaving to get a bite to eat or to stretch their legs by walking up and down the hallway.

The tests are completed. The doctor doing the spinal tap tells me I'll probably have headaches from the air injected into my spinal cord. Right now I just feel groggy as I lie in the hospital bed on my left side. I'm glad it is over.

Dad gets up and starts pacing, walks out into the hallway and then back into the room. His brow is furrowed. Mom asks me if I want fresh water. She comes over to me and holds my hand. Dad sits down in the big leather chair. He is silent. Not more than a couple of minutes later, he gets up and walks out of the room again. He returns and stands just inside the door, staring straight ahead, but does not focus on me or anything else in the room. I have seen this pattern before. Dad cares intensely but does not communicate well when dealing with illness in our family.

"Dad," I say, "you're making me nervous. I know how much you care about me, but all I feel is worry. That bothers me. It would be better for me if you leave. I'm going to be okay."

Mom gets up, gives me a kiss on the cheek, and puts on her coat. She retrieves Dad's coat and gives it to him. He comes over to me, leans down, and gives me a kiss on my cheek, saying nothing.

"You need to rest, Arlene," Mom says. "We will go for a walk, have dinner, and come back to see how you're doing before visiting hours end." She puts her arm through Dad's and they walk out the door.

The neurologist contacts Dad at the motel with the test results. Inconclusive. That one word is what Dad says to me, "inconclusive." No drum roll. No sirens. Just a vague word of uncertainty. I'm not sure why I don't ask Dad what they tested me for. A brain tumor? A serious nerve condition? Maybe I don't ask because I'm young and want to pretend nothing is wrong.

I want an answer, but most of all I want to feel my legs again.

— CHAPTER 3 —

Derailed

I'm wishing and wishing the feeling will return to my legs and feet. Wishing doesn't make it so. They're still numb.

On Saturday, Mom and I head back to Minneapolis. Kind and nurturing, Mom shops, stocks my refrigerator with chicken, hamburger meat, milk, and lettuce, and then takes off for the long drive home.

The next day throws me into a tunnel, and I'm not yet seeing light at the end. My head swirls, not sure what to focus on, not sure what will come next. I want to try to make the next step happen, rather than have it happen to me. *What if I can't? What if my dream of being a leader ends before it has barely begun?*

I call my boss, tell him my tests are over, with inconclusive results, and my legs and feet are still numb. I don't know yet when I can return to work. He asks me to check in with him in a week. My brother is coming next weekend and it will be good to talk with him. He is a second-year medical student at the University of Iowa. We didn't get to talk when I was in the city undergoing tests. David and I rumbled and tumbled when we were kids, literally getting into physical fights that got rough, but we also rode our bikes side by side, played catch, and snuggled up in one stuffed chair together when we watched a scary movie like *The Blob*. On the quiet and pensive side, David has always supported me without pushing me one way or another. It will be great to ask him what might be wrong. He might not know for sure, but he is smart and is steeped in studying medicine.

On late Friday afternoon, David arrives, clutches me in a big hug, and asks how I'm doing. He sits down in the comfy green chair and I stretch out on the couch. I'm exhausted, even with so little physical activity. The tests wiped me out, I tell him, and my boss wants to hear from me next week.

"What do I tell him about a time for returning? I don't have a clue," I say.

"You might not want to hear this, but your body will tell you when you are ready. It could take a while," he says. I feel discouraged. *Why can't my body spring back just as quickly as my feeling left? Maybe it can. I want to believe that.*

It could take a while. I try to let those words sink in. I want to feel some progress. *How can I make a decision based on not knowing anything?* On Sunday morning when I get out of bed, my right foot hits the floor. I feel the outside of my right foot! David cooks scrambled eggs and bacon for breakfast, and we toast this occasion of feeling in my foot as we clank our coffee mugs together. He leaves, and I am left wondering again.

Regaining feeling is like water coming out of a faucet, one drip at a time. One spot, then in patches, feeling returns, first on the outside of my feet, then on the outside of my legs. Increased feeling doesn't come every day. It's unpredictable. I can walk but tire easily and am not one-hundred-percent sure of my footing. My assuredness in walking wanes, and I don't have confidence yet that I can walk outside to the end of my block.

As the last weeks of December arrive, the thought of getting on a bus, standing on my feet during twelve-hour hectic workdays, and maintaining stamina to be an effective employee overwhelms me. If I take even a month more time off work, I will have missed a critical chunk of my training. Although my head resists, my direction is clear. I call my boss and reluctantly tell him I cannot return to my management trainee position. Derailed just three months into my promising career, I'm filled with disappointment. *What do I do with this uncertain body? How will I earn a living so I can live on my own?* I shudder at the thought of being forced to go *home*, live off Mom and Dad, because I can't take care of myself.

◆ ◆ ◆

After a few days of feeling *This isn't fair*, my let's-move-forward self swings into action. My brain craves stimulation. *What can I do using my head since my body is not at one hundred percent?* I love academic challenges, so I'll take a course at the University of Minnesota. Perusing the course catalog, my eyes focus on "Communications." I begin a rhetorical criticism course, earn some money by working in the university library, sitting at a desk with a stack of books in front of me, putting a label with the book title and Dewey decimal number on the book spine. It's a far cry from Dayton's, but it keeps me busy and gives time for my body to repair.

I keep asking myself what I can do next with my brain and not have to depend on my body. Graduate school pops up front and center in my mind. After work is completed at the library, my attention zeroes in on researching grad schools. Since I have a degree in journalism, expanding my knowledge in communications areas appeals to me. Group and organizational dynamics fascinate me, how people relate with one another in small and large groups as they work at their jobs. With expansive research across the country's universities and colleges, I discover an innovative graduate program in communications and business at the University of Kansas. Even though I've never been to the campus, or to the state, for that matter, I apply and get accepted. Things are looking up as the trees bud, signaling the arrival of spring and new beginnings.

I'll be entering graduate school in the fall and now all feeling is back in my legs and feet.

— CHAPTER 4 —

Gaining Confidence

Graduate school begins in the fall of 1971. My one-bedroom furnished apartment is half of a stand-alone duplex and close enough to walk to all my classes. My energy is high and I can walk with vigor. That day a year ago when I lost feeling from my waist down is behind me. I'm hoping it was a fluke, but since there was no definitive diagnosis, a little voice sometimes whispers, *Will it happen again?*

I try to push the worries out of my head and concentrate on my studies and my friends. My good friend Dena enters a graduate program at KU a year later. We roomed together at Iowa, played bridge, and, as students do, tried to figure out our place in the dizzying world of free love, the Vietnam War, and the scary military lottery for our friends. Then we ended up in Minneapolis at the same time. Dena has just left her teaching position in Upstate New York and is trying to figure out what to do next. She has enrolled in a graduate program for special education. We sit in coffeehouses and reminisce about how we each led organizations in college, me as the president of my sorority and her as the head of the campus sorority system. Now I am putting labels on book binders and she is working at the Manpower temporary work agency. We laugh and say we are "in between" important endeavors.

Kathie, another friend from Iowa, is in Kansas City, training to be a flight attendant for TWA. One day, I drive thirty-five miles in my yellow Chevy Nova to visit Kathie at work. Once I'm inside the front door of the Training Center, the scene causes me to stop and stare, a gigantic lobby with a light stone floor and accents of white marble. A long *up* escalator carries three women with straight dark hair, in navy jackets and skirts. I feel like I'm on a movie set, with each cast member smartly dressed in her uniform, hair coiffed, just enough makeup, nails perfectly painted. I feel self-conscious in my wide-wale corduroy pants and long-sleeve shirt.

I ask the receptionist to call Kathie, and a few minutes later, I spot her coming down that long escalator to greet me. We run toward each other and embrace tightly. The tinge of discomfort I feel as an underdressed grad student fades away. With Kathie, I get a glimpse of a glamorous industry, behind the scenes, which I would not have had the opportunity to experience otherwise.

Kathie, Dena, and I are spreading our wings as young professional women. Most of my college friends did not marry soon after graduation; in fact, being in a serious romantic relationship was not a priority. Friendships were. The dynamics on campus shifted during our sophomore year. The norm changed from alcohol to marijuana, from clean-shaven men to beards, from women wearing A-line skirts to bell-bottom pants. Among Dena, Kathie, and our other friends, caring and supporting one another were sacrosanct.

◆ ◆ ◆

The following Monday, I'm walking home from my organizational design class. My two books are lodged under my right arm, my elbow pressed into my side, helping to hold the books securely. Suddenly I realize my skin feels funny where my elbow presses against my side.

Putting down my books once inside my apartment, I shed my jacket and explore my right side. I press my fingers around my flesh. A semicircle, from the front center of my stomach around to the center of my back, is numb. It's an inch or so in depth and only on my right side.

Oh no. Is this related to losing my feeling from the waist down in Minneapolis? Like air being popped out of a balloon, my energy droops. I start to awfulize. *I'm going to lose my feeling again. I'm going to lose it. This can't be happening.* I push away the tears welling up in my eyes and take off on a long walk, a fast one.

The next morning, my right side feels normal. With a sigh of relief that numbness didn't go to my feet, I go about my day.

◆ ◆ ◆

My courses finish by the end of 1972 and what lies ahead is defending my master's thesis. I'm offered a research position at KU, starting after graduation in May, where I can earn money and work on my PhD. But I'm eager to work in a business, where the pace is fast and achieving results is rewarded. I contact a family friend, a business consultant in Chicago. Timing is great, as the National Restaurant Association, one of his clients, is hiring master-level graduates for a big research project. I apply, interview, and get the job.

The research skills I developed in grad school give me increased marketability. With Dena, Kathie, and I all focused on our professional careers, we support one another in moving forward. Our many conversations, reassuring one another of our competence and taking a risk for a new job, make the "yes" response to a new position easier.

I'm excited, thinking about living in Chicago. Big cities have appealed to me as far back as childhood. Every year on the day after Thanksgiving, our family of five arose at 4:45 a.m. for the hour-and-a-half Amtrak train ride to Chicago. We spent the day looking at Marshall Field's elaborate window displays, waiting in line to see Santa Claus, and eating lunch in the Walnut Room by the gigantic Christmas tree. I loved the escalators, the people rushing around, the excitement of the big city. As we grew older, Mom and Dad brought us to Chicago to see live theater like *The Music Man* and *Fiddler on the Roof.* I liked our dinner afterward at Fritzel's, where dinner plates were topped with a domed cover and, in one dramatic move, the waiters lifted off those covers to reveal our meal.

When I first imagined being in Kansas, my picture was of Matt Dillon swinging the door open into a bar, as in one of my favorite TV shows *Gunsmoke.* My graduate school experience has been quite the opposite, rich in intellectual stimulation and in building my confidence. Now with my newly formed confidence, I'll be headed to the bustling streets of Chicago.

◆ ◆ ◆

Even with an exciting new job ahead, a little anxiety lurks in the back of my mind. I'm still afraid that my feet and legs might go numb or maybe worse.

What if my career is stalled again by my body?

— CHAPTER 5 —

Barbra on My Fire Escape

In the spring of 1973, I move to Chicago and begin my job as a researcher for the National Restaurant Association. We are part of a one-year contract from the US Department of Labor, studying promotional opportunities for entry-level workers in the food service industry. Generally, they are nonexistent. The long workdays don't faze me, as my energy is high and stamina strong. I walk twenty minutes to work and love bicycling along the Lake Michigan shoreline on my days off.

My sixth-floor apartment near Lincoln Park Zoo is perfect for me. The tiny kitchen contains a gold-colored gas range, refrigerator, and small countertop. It has French doors leading out to a wrought-iron fire escape, which winds down from the top of the building to the ground. I imagine Barbra Streisand standing on a rung, right outside my door, blasting out "Hello, Dolly." I love Barbra. Bobby, my good friend from the University of Iowa, is her biggest fan.

Bobby and I met through mutual friends in college and often socialized together, not only at parties but also in serious discussions about what kind of life we were preparing for and what the impact of the social unrest spurred on by the war meant for us, our friends, and the future of the country.

◆ ◆ ◆

Bobby is Mr. Personality, endearing, a person whom others gravitate toward. He is fun, generous, and adventurous. My time with Bobby, Dena, Kathie, and other close friends in undergrad times, plus Dena and Kathie while in Kansas at grad school, reinforced the importance of friendship and authenticity in my life, being with me to listen and share stories and angst about the national scene. *Who can I count on to lay out my fears to? To listen to my doubts about life having any meaning? Is moral character completely absent with students being shot, Martin Luther King assassinated?* It was an unsettling time in the country during my college years, and my friends meant everything.

Bobby lives in Chicago and we, along with our group of eight Chicago friends, spend evenings together, listening to Barbra's records for hours. It's not all laughs, though. These days, we gather in Chinatown to eat and celebrate the end of the US involvement in the Vietnam War, marked by the signing of the Paris Peace Accords in late January. The first prisoners of war have just been released. We intersperse laughter with serious conversation because the news continues to remind us of ongoing trouble and violence. Patty Hearst was just kidnapped by the Symbionese Liberation Army. How can that possibly have a good outcome? And news reporters continue to broadcast and write editorials about the Watergate scandal. It has been months since top White House aides resigned as a result of their involvement. Pressure continues on President Nixon. His announcement in November last year, "I am not a crook," continues to pop up on TV. None of my friends believe him. Nor do I.

In January 1974, an executive recruiter contacts me and is very encouraging about possibilities for, as he says, "a very bright, young professional woman." He asks me about my goals. My response comes easily, as I want to make a difference, lead in a company where I can bring caring and fairness to employees at all levels. I want to get rid of outdated, punitive policies as I did with the social rules for women on campus at the University of Iowa.

In February, I fly to New Orleans to present a research paper at the annual conference of the International Communication Association, my final commitment from grad school. This paper is a summary of research that led to my master's thesis.

My research looks at a new form of organizational design called a "task force," where a group of people come together to solve a problem, and then the group dissolves. My research partner and I look at the flow of communication in the group, how trust is created, and what process is used to make decisions. This task force concept is innovative, brand new. How exciting for me to conduct groundbreaking research, then present the outcome to an international group of scholars and businesspeople.

Arriving home from New Orleans, I find an unexpected letter in my mailbox from the director of training for United Airlines. He invites me to come to their executive offices to talk with him about a research position. I go. Although the National Restaurant Association offers me a promotion, United offers me a job, which I accept. My work as a research specialist for the airline starts in May at their executive offices in Elk Grove Village, a Chicago suburb.

It's great that I can stay in my cozy apartment, singing "People" along with Barbra and my Chicago friends, which brings joy and laughter into my busy life.

— CHAPTER 6 —

Flying High

Just two weeks after I start my new job in Chicago, my work travel begins and goes at warp speed for all of 1974. About 70 percent of this first year in my job is spent on the West Coast, mainly in San Francisco at United's sprawling airplane maintenance center. The famous hills, Golden Gate Park, and sparkling bay become regular sights. It's fun because Kathie lives in the Marina area and we frequently see each other. Whether coincidence or meant to be, Kathie's and my life continue to connect, from Iowa to Kansas to San Francisco and even travel as we spent a lovely five days earlier that year in Hawaii.

Within two years I'm promoted to management education representative. Based at headquarters in Chicago, I begin to work on performance review programs for supervisors, managers, and directors and hone my training and speaking skills. Key people start to know my name, know that if they take one of my classes, it will be well worth their while and fun, too.

Although young, I don't want to burn out, plus the patch of numbness on my right leg in 1976 reminds me I need to take care. I make sure to take needed vacation breaks and use my travel benefits to fly to remote destinations, including a two-week visit to Israel, Paris, and Rome and another standby trip to Rio de Janeiro for four fun days on the gorgeous beaches. In the midst of my travels, I am recruited hard and offered another promotion. Maybe the hard sell is because this will require relocating.

Now in the spring of 1977 after flying east out of O'Hare an hour earlier, I gaze out the window at the puffy white clouds. My mind wanders. *Did you always want to work for an airline? Are you a flight attendant?* are two common questions I'm asked. And I'm used to people at parties telling me their lost bag stories. I'm vaguely aware of the sound of the airplane's landing gear. *Am I moving too fast? As a Midwesterner, will I fit into the East Coast, into the fast pace of New York?* I am a little nervous, but what an adventure this might be. We hit the runway at LaGuardia for a perfect landing, which I hope to experience in New York City.

— CHAPTER 7 —

Walking Fast

Every workday morning, I walk to the office, one of the thousands moving with purpose on the sidewalks of Manhattan. I am grateful to have strong legs and no symptoms of numbness in my body. Chicago is a big city, but this is so much bigger and on an island. We have to go over or under water to get here. Everything seems vertical. Very early on, I was told not to look up. That is what the tourists do. You can always pick out the tourists because they are gawking upward. I walk most places. If my destination is too far, I jump on the subway or take the M3 bus going up Madison Avenue. This is a city that walks and walks fast. Everything is fast. The electric energy on the streets is palpable.

Manager of Training and Development is my new title, working for the Eastern Division operational headquarters of United Airlines offices on the twenty-second floor in the McGraw-Hill building in Midtown Manhattan. I am the only woman manager and at least twenty years younger than all the male managers. The unspoken uniform is a suit, white shirt, and tie for the men and a navy suit jacket and A-line skirt for me. I wear two-and-a-half-inch-heeled shoes to play the part and keep them on from the moment I leave my apartment in the morning until I return in the evening. My long fingernails with deep red polish cap off my look. Even though I supervise a staff and direct major employee programs, when I tell people I work for an airline, they ask if I'm a flight attendant or assume I'm in a secretarial role.

Days zoom by, filled with meetings, returning phone calls, reviewing budgets, checking in with regional managers, and supervising my four direct reports. I rarely go out for lunch. Usually I grab a sandwich from the coffee shop in the lobby and eat it at my desk while doing more work. My briefcase is always full in the evening when I walk out of the office, carrying with me papers that need to be read in preparation for meetings the next morning.

♦ ♦ ♦

I walk to my one-bedroom apartment located at 30 Park Avenue, on the corner of 36th Street. From my sixth-floor bedroom window, I can see the top third of the Empire State Building. It makes me think of the movie *An Affair to Remember*, romantic and iconic. So many things in Manhattan remind me of movies—the sea of yellow taxis racing down Fifth Avenue, Prometheus at Rockefeller Center, the fast-walking crowds of people shoulder to shoulder, streaming down Broadway or across 42nd Street—all favorite background scenes for plotlines. I have always loved movies and occasionally get the chance here to stop on a street corner to watch a film crew shooting a movie scene.

My living room is welcoming and comfortable. My orange-striped sofa from Chicago sits on the orange shag carpet that is cushy to walk or sit on. What a fascinating experience apartment shopping was. Many apartments here are tiny and expensive and dark because the small windows face another high-rise that blocks the sunlight. When looking around, I laughed when I saw an ad for an apartment with *bathtub in kitchen*. Really? I had to go take a look. Yep, a board placed over the kitchen tub serves as a counter-top. You take it off to bathe.

On the weekends my social life is hopping. I start dating Richard, a six-foot-tall, slender man with sandy hair who works at Goldman Sachs. We usually dress up in work clothes when we go out because he likes his members-only club in Midtown. Richard likes mingling with his work partners, developing social and business relationships. I find, though, there is little separation between work and play. Plus, it is smokey, and the thing I really dislike is that women can only be in the restaurant and one other room. In getting to know Richard better, he seems too stuffy for me, a really nice guy, thirty years old, but not enough fun. This relationship is not going to last very long.

A sorority sister friend from Iowa, Lorraine, who has lived in New York City since graduation, and I go to movies, eat Chinese food, and laugh a lot. Dena comes to visit and it is always like no time has passed. So does Bobby. In fact, Bobby is talking about moving to New York City in a couple of years. I meet a man named Joe. He loves to go clubbing and we head out on Friday evening at 10:00 when the *real* nightlife is just starting to gear up. Joe is about five feet eight with dark, curly hair and beautiful blue eyes. He looks like he could be a family member in the *Godfather* movies. He is from New Jersey, definitely an East Coaster all the way. When I tell him I graduated from the University of Iowa, he gets Iowa confused with

Ohio. He is not the only one. I am learning many locals know of New York and Los Angeles, and nothing in between. The Midwest is a big void. My interest wanes with Joe. I don't know if I'm not finding men to date who are compatible with me or if I'm just not that interested in dating. I'm not pining after a certain man, a soul mate. It's just fun and interesting to meet new people.

The fast pace suits me well. I am finding my way, finding my rhythm in the Big Apple. I am happy, confident, independent, and where I want to be. All doors seem open as I walk into my future here.

— CHAPTER 8 —

Locker Room Musings

Now a little over a year into my job, in the spring of 1978, I'm in my groove as intensity and pressure remain constant—deadlines, meetings, employee problems, budgets. It's never-ending. I struggle to allow myself to take breaks, let loose, have fun. Yet I know it's too much stress, too much work. I have to exercise my body more. I begin looking for exercise classes that have low-impact movements, stretching, and maybe a little weightlifting. I discover a health club on 42nd Street between Fifth and Sixth Avenues, close to Bryant Park, that's on my path home from work.

I join. Quickly, my favorite instructor is Melody. She is full of energy, with short, dark brown hair and huge, expressive eyes that remind me of Judy Garland. I like that she does not seem to take herself too seriously. I feel good in her classes and they make me forget work for a while.

On a Thursday after class, I am changing my clothes in the locker room. I am amazed that some women do not have any modesty and parade around naked, with their makeup bag in one hand and a towel draped over an arm. It's so far from the Midwestern, private modesty that I was taught. Is this an adult woman thing that I am just now being exposed to? These women seem casual and unconcerned. I'm the one who feels uncomfortable and anxious with my culture shock.

Two women sit on a bench near me, with a terry-cloth towel wrapped around each body and one around each of their heads.

"You know, Marie, my therapist says I should set more boundaries. I just tell everybody what I think," one woman says loudly.

"Well, Barbara, my therapist, oh I just love her, keeps asking me why I am guarded about my feelings when I talk to Richard. I need a little of you in me," Marie says back to her, waving her hands up in the air as she talks.

"It has been fifteen years that I have been in therapy," Barbara goes on. "I feel depressed, then happy, then down again. You'd think I'd be over that by now."

I feel like I am in the middle of a Woody Allen movie! These women are going on and on about their neuroses. This must be an East Coast or maybe a New York City thing. In my Midwest upbringing, I was taught to keep my feelings pretty much to myself. Tough it out. Other people have worse problems. Dad did not even like the word *therapist* or *psychiatrist*. He thought it was a sign of weakness to see someone just for the purpose of talking. At least, that's my interpretation of hearing him say he wouldn't pay money for a therapist. That sticks with me because I rarely talk about any personal sadness, disappointment, or anger I feel.

My clothes changed, I'm ready to head for home, wondering what I should fix for dinner.

As I step out the front door of the health club, it is dark and I feel a chill in the air that lingers in these spring days. Light comes from the streetlights, headlights of cars and taxis, and illuminated store windows. I turn left. Suddenly, the feeling goes in and out of my right leg and the skin on my right ankle twitches. *Oh no.* Like intermittent static on a radio, feeling, no feeling, feeling. I have no dial to turn to bring the frequency back to normal. *Breathe, Arlene, breathe.* I stop in front of a Duane Reade drugstore and freeze. What do I do? How can I manage here in Manhattan if I don't have feeling, can't walk? If Dad knew, he would probably tell me to return to the Midwest, come closer to home, where he could connect me with great doctors.

I don't want to leave. I not only want to be a successful businesswoman in a tough airline industry but also want to do it in the Big Apple. Frank Sinatra had it right, "If you can make it here, you can make it anywhere." This city envelops me with energy, with possibilities, with the chance to shine as the first female manager in the New York office. But something is wrong in my body. I'm terrified that I'll be out of commission for months if this goes like my extreme loss of feeling eight years ago in Minneapolis.

Bringing my attention back to the present, I cautiously take a step forward. The bottom of my foot feels normal. Another step forward. The strength in my legs seems good. With confidence now that I can do it, I quickly walk six blocks to my apartment.

The feeling returns to normal in two days. I'm on edge, though, uneasy because the feeling in and out of my skin bodes potential danger ahead. It's not *if* but *when* the next episode will hit.

CHAPTER 9

Walking Slowly

A s I exit my office building, a stiff wind hits my face. When I cross over Fifth Avenue on 42nd Street, my right leg feels like it is giving out from under me. Is there a crack in the sidewalk, a stone that I stepped on that threw me off-balance? My left arm and hand tingle. My heartbeat quickens. I stop and stand near a store doorway for a few minutes. I feel weak all over. Six blocks to go. *I can get there. I can do it.* I walk slowly, tentatively, as walkers buzz by me. Everything speeds up around me, moving faster and faster. Not me. I seem to be moving in slow motion. I breathe a sigh of relief when my apartment building comes into view.

◆ ◆ ◆

It's been obvious for months that I need to see a neurologist. *What am I waiting for? Am I in denial, hoping for my thirty-year-old body to rebound?* Yes, I am, but that little voice in my head isn't reliable. My rational self takes over; I do my due diligence research and make an appointment.

In the next week, getting off the bus at East 72nd Street, I face my destination, medical offices associated with New York Hospital. I will be right on time for my 9:00 a.m. appointment with a neurologist, Frank P.

Dr. P, average height, light-colored hair, and a pleasant smile, extends his hand to greet me. After telling him about my current symptoms, he asks me, "Have you had any previous symptoms of tingling or weakness in your legs?"

"Yes, a couple brief episodes that disappeared, but . . ." I glance down to the floor. *Should I keep talking, tell him? Do I have to recall that terrible experience in Minneapolis?*

"But what?"

"I lost the feeling from my waist down one afternoon, eight years ago."

His eyes widen and he purses his lips.

"Let me examine you," he says, pointing to the bland medical table with white sterile paper on top. "Look straight at me. Take your index finger, extend it out, then back to touch your nose. Again. Again. Now, look at me and cover one eye. How many fingers do you see?" These tests are familiar, similar to what I experienced in Iowa City several years ago. Fine to follow his finger, but what will it show? I did this before with no results, no diagnosis. I'm afraid I'm going to hear "we're not sure what this is." Another disappointment.

Next he gently taps the outside of my right knee with a tuning fork. Then the other one. He hits the tuning fork with his hand, then puts it up against the sole of my left foot.

"Do you feel anything?" he asks.

"Tingling." My eyes drift to stare across the room at the wall behind the sink. *Am I passing these tests? How is this helping me get to what's wrong?*

"Okay. Good. Now step down and stand facing me. Close your eyes." My eyelids close and I feel wobbly; I say that, even though the doctor can obviously see. After a minute or so, he has me open my eyes and walk to the door, one heel in front of the opposite toes. This test I'm definitely not passing.

"We need to do a CT scan. That is the only way to get at a diagnosis. In the meantime, I am going to prescribe oral prednisone, a fourteen-day regimen. It is important to follow directions precisely. You slowly cut down on strength and taper off. It is important that you do not just stop abruptly."

"What does this prednisone do?" I ask, thinking this does not sound good.

"It helps stop and hopefully lower inflammation," he answers. "That is what we need to do."

"What are the possibilities for what is wrong?" I ask.

"It seems neurological, but I do not want to conjecture prematurely. Let's wait until I see the test results."

♦ ♦ ♦

I schedule and go through the test ten days later, going to the lab by myself and keeping it to myself. I tell no one. I schedule an 8:00 a.m. appointment so I am not too late into the office.

"Inconclusive," I hear from Dr. P a few days later. "Keep in touch with me so we can track your symptoms and see if the prednisone works."

Why can't they find out what the problem is rather than stringing me along? And if they don't know what's wrong and can't make it better, then what?

The prednisone causes me to have spurts of energy at the wrong times. Like 3:00 a.m., when I wake up, eyes wide open, not able to fall back to sleep. The dosage ends, and in a couple of weeks, I feel much better. In a month, the symptoms are gone. That doesn't bring me comfort. I have to work every day at pushing *when will this return* out of my mind. Some nights I wake up from my sleep in a panic because I've been dreaming I am in a wheelchair.

Two months later, a familiar scene repeats itself. Walking home on the cement streets of New York City, my legs feel like they will not hold me up. Extreme weakness in both legs, plus sharp pain as if needles are poked into me. I stop, move close to a storefront to think about what I should do.

I am only a block from where Melody is teaching. I will go there and see her. I'm not strong enough to take her class, but I need her company. I'm afraid my legs might not hold me upright.

It takes every ounce of energy I have to put one foot in front of the other. My balance is iffy. *Are people staring at me? Do I look like I've had too much to drink?* I arrive at the health club, and once inside the door, I go for a chair close to the check-in desk.

"Is Melody here?" I ask the attendant.

"Yes. She is downstairs. Class starts in about twenty-five minutes."

"Could you call her and tell her Arlene wants to see her?"

I make my way to the top of the stairs and hear Melody's voice. Her face appears in my view.

"Come on down, Arlene."

"I'm not sure I can. My legs are so weak they may not hold me. I don't want to fall."

Rather than panicking, Melody remains calm and reassuring. "Come on down," she urges. "You can do it."

Slowly I sit down on the top step and scoot down on my behind, one step at a time.

As I get to the bottom step, I'm totally exhausted. Melody runs over, bends down, and gives me a big hug. My body goes limp. I am so relieved not to be alone.

"You made it, my friend. I'll help you." Her hug feels like Mom's did when she held me tight as a kid during thunderstorms. Her embrace made me feel everything would be okay.

◆ ◆ ◆

Mom has always been there for me. When I was six years old, she included me in decorating Christmas cookies. When I spilled sprinkles, red hots, or icing on the floor, without missing a beat as she continued to stir the dough, she'd hand me a wet cloth and tell me to wipe up what I spilled. She would say, "That's okay, it happens to all of us." Giving me my own summertime task to shuck ears of sweet corn and snap off the ends of green beans was so special. She trusted me. Comforting me at nine years old when a girl knocked a book out of my hand and said I was so smart and she hated me for it. Mom listened, gave me a hug, and told me some girls can be mean. "You're great just the way you are. And it's a good thing to be smart." And sewing tiny labels with my name on them to towels and sheets when I went off to college. And staying by my side during and after my CT scan in Iowa City.

Melody teaches her class, changes her clothes, and returns with a smile on her face to cheer me up. We talk for twenty minutes, and then, when I feel I am ready, I grab her arm, holding tightly, and we slowly walk back to my apartment.

CHAPTER 10

Your Body Doesn't Lie

A week later I feel more stable with better balance, so much better that I know I can go to my health club, get down the stairs, and attend Melody's class. What a strange condition I have. One day I can barely get down steps, and a couple of days later I bounce back and feel fine. Right now I am feeling achy and stiff from so much sitting at my office desk and at night on my couch in my apartment. I am ready and excited to return to Melody's class.

"Your body doesn't lie," Melody says as she leads stretching exercises for six of us women in colorful leotards. I ruminate over these words and think, *What if I listened to my body the way I listen to my brain?* Have I been living too long from my neck up?

"Let's stretch our backs at the ballet bar," she adds, walking over to the bar to show us how to do it. "Stretching is a must," she says, as she stresses in every class. *This feels so good, my muscles relaxing, stresses of the day melting away. I'm just starting to get it, that stretching doesn't just feel good; it's also restorative and necessary for my body to be healthy.*

Melody exudes energy and a zest for life. We hit it off, me, the aspiring corporate leader, and her, the free spirit, bigger-than-life extrovert. Her class and her encouragement help me deal with my leg weakness, tingling, and occasional fogginess from that powerful prednisone. Right now, our relationship centers mostly on class and maybe a chat afterward. I do feel a bond developing between us. Melody helps me relax and let go and I wonder what intrigues her about me. Maybe it's my business acumen and determination to do and live big. She is listening to my encouragement for her to open her own business.

◆ ◆ ◆

During the next several months, I continue to take classes, and college friends frequently pop into my picture. Thomas, a good friend from the University of Iowa days, visits me, as does my old friend Lorraine. We had many mutual friends in college but never dated. But during his visits to New York, something changes, and we are dating. Long distance isn't easy, but we want to give it a whirl. I admire the kindness, wit, and intellect inside his tall six-foot-two frame.

In the midst of the fun and laughs, I realize he is getting serious about me, wanting a longer-term relationship. I wish we could just focus on the present. He is caring but doesn't get it when I say my body feels like needles are pressed into my skin. Touch can be painful, can feel like the needles are digging deeper into my skin. My physical distancing, pushing him away sometimes, makes him feel rejected. I try to explain. It does not seem to work. Through it all, we are seeing each other less, talking less on the phone. Is it due to body pain I feel with intimacy? Could it be my rejection of Thomas? My body's rejection of men? I just need to find a partner who will accept and understand my pain.

◆ ◆ ◆

Melody gets it. She is teaching me to pay attention to my body. Our friendship is growing. I would not have imagined we would click on such a personal level. We laugh, sitting on my orange couch shoulder to shoulder, commiserating about her growing business, her energetic classes, and how we both seek a full, exciting life. I am her reasoned, stable side; she is my exuberance, my letting go of inhibitions, my guide to a better body.

"Your body does not lie," I repeat to Melody as we sit upright on her bottom bunk. "I have been thinking about that a lot. For me, my mind has always provided many options, powered me through."

"But, Arlene, your body is always talking to you, even now," she says, taking my hand to admire my long, red fingernails. "Your mind talks to you too, but sometimes it tricks you," she adds. *Hm, it tricks me. I have to think about that one.*

We stop, look at each other, not saying a thing, then break out into laughter as we throw our arms around each other for a tight, reassuring hug.

While I might want to explore a more intimate relationship with Melody, she is involved with a couple of people and I know enough not to pursue it. Still, our friendship is something I cherish.

– CHAPTER 11 –

On the Streets
of Manhattan

Standing on a street corner, unsteady and trying to keep myself upright, I have twenty seconds to cross the street. The light will turn green, the cars will accelerate quickly, and I need to get my body across the street to the other side. What if my legs can't move fast enough and the light turns yellow, then red when I'm in the middle of the crosswalk? Can I make it across without getting hit by a car?

How could it happen at such a young age, thirty years old, that my life suddenly flashes in front of me—as a high school basketball star swishing the net with my jump shot, as a journalism student running speedily to the newsroom to submit an exclusive story . . . all in my mind's eye as I stand on this street corner trying to keep myself steady on my feet?

The light turns green. Twenty seconds flashes at me from the streetlight. I step off the curb. People scurry in front and beside me. A sea of faces comes toward me as the crowd on the other side crosses over. *I can do this. I can make it. I do not want to fall.* I slowly put one foot in front of the other, concentrating hard on each step. My legs aren't as sturdy as they usually are. My right ankle is weak. *Keep moving, Arlene, one foot in front of the other.* What if my legs collapse? What if my legs won't move and I'm stuck in the middle of the street?

Seven seconds left. The light is going to change and the cars will accelerate, zoom through the intersection toward me. I can't count on them to slow down for me. Oh, my God, can I make it? Mustering every ounce of available energy, I will myself to keep walking. Just as the light turns red, my right foot steps up on the curb. I make it without a second to spare.

My body trembles. My eyes water. I'm so relieved but don't feel safe because my body feels weak. My eyes dart to a bench a few feet away. I make it to the bench and plop down. Safety, for a few moments. I let out an audible breath. I'm scared because I'm not safe on the streets. And I'm exhausted from crossing the street.

My mind races as I sit on the bench. Making it across the street doesn't feel like a victory. It took every ounce of energy and total focus to cross one street corner. That twenty-second crossing seemed so long. A blaring car horn throws me back into the present. *I have to get up, get myself home.* Slowly I stand up, take a step, then another step, moving with determination toward the finish line, home. I make it. Upon entering my apartment, I head straight to the couch to stretch out. I fall into a deep sleep.

Over the next couple of weeks, I ruminate about where I am—in a chronic state of wobbliness, not being able to fully control one leg, sometimes both. My career is flying high and my body is falling apart.

On the street, people look at me. *Are they wondering what is wrong with me? Do I look unstable like the scarecrow in* The Wizard of Oz? My skin, hair, clothes, my entire appearance seems *normal*, I think, but I do not feel that way. Inside I feel disfigured like Quasimodo. I must stand out in the crowd, hunched over, unsteady on my feet. People must be thinking, *She is a little weird. What is her problem?*

♦ ♦ ♦

Something needs to change so I feel stable out on the streets. I consider buying a cane to steady me but don't fully embrace my own idea. A month later, I am in Chicago and walk into Marshall Field's. I'm still thinking about a cane and decide to take a look, to see what's available. Swallowing my ego and desire to believe that my body is okay, I convince myself to shop for a cane. As much as I don't want to be a thirty-year-old with a cane, it will bring me relief and confidence for those times when my walking ability is compromised. I spend over an hour browsing, testing out metal and wooden canes and walking sticks. I want the right one, one that is distinguished and proud. It will be my prop, like an actor uses in a play. I want the right prop to fit into the scene so it looks like it belongs there. My eyes zero in on a beautiful, brown wood cane with a curved handle and finely polished surface. I do not have to look further. This is the one and I have no second thoughts.

♦ ♦ ♦

While I'm back in New York City, my cane has become my friend, in my hand and at my side when I need it, giving me courage and strength to keep moving up, down, and across the street. I realize people on the street are more intentional about giving me space when they see my cane and do not follow or pass by me closely. Some even smile and hold a door open for me. I have fondness and warm feelings for these women and men I encounter, whose names I will never know. I feel cared for and accepted out on the sidewalks and streets.

But I am nervous because, with my career ascending, I don't feel the same about my cane in the office. I am afraid it might signal weakness, might cause my boss or division head to ask themselves, "Is she up to managing this fast-paced, chaotic environment?" When I walk into the office with my cane, I underplay its purpose. If someone asks me why I have it, I just brush it off or say I have a minor nerve-ending problem and am getting good care. That satisfies. I don't get any follow-up questions.

◆ ◆ ◆

A month after buying my cane in Chicago, I go for a prescheduled follow-up CT scan. It lasts about twenty-five minutes. I am glad to be out of that cold room. I walk down the bright hallway to the dressing room. I change my clothes, leave the hospital, and walk slowly, aided by my cane. I am on my way home by bus, not going to the office. I took a personal day today, which is a nice company benefit to have.

A week later, I am sitting alone in the familiar office of Dr. P. I like his kind, patient approach and his ability to translate complex medical terms into plain English. I fidget in the waiting room chair because I'm anxious, terrified that my condition is fatal, a brain tumor.

"So, how are you today?" he asks.

"Not great. My head feels foggy and my thinking is not clear," I respond. I have lost all sense of what *normal* feels like.

"There are a few possibilities for a diagnosis," he says, pushing his glasses up his nose. *Is he keeping something from me, vague because he doesn't want to tell me it's fatal?* "My team has been going through a process of elimination with your case. It is not Parkinson's disease. It is not a brain tumor." *Not a brain tumor? What other fatal condition might I have?* I stare directly at the doctor, trying my best to focus. Pen in hand, I am ready to take notes on my little, lined spiral pad of paper. *Is he being vague because he doesn't want to give bad news to someone so young?*

"Based on all the tests you have been through and our medical team's knowledge and experience, we are about ninety percent sure it is multiple sclerosis."

"Am I headed for a wheelchair?" pops out of my mouth. *Oh no. My activity will be severely limited. My body will continue to deteriorate. My social life will end. I'm just getting started in NYC and have so much life to live.*

The combination of powerful steroids and uncertainty has filled my days for so long. Finally, I am receiving some practical words that might bring more certainty, a more definite course of action.

"That is not an automatic conclusion," he says, now leaning forward, resting his folded arms on his desk, looking right into my eyes. "There are different levels of severity with multiple sclerosis, or MS." I look down and fill the page with two big letters—M S.

I raise my head and face the doctor as he continues, "MS is a condition in which there is damage to the myelin sheath, the protective coating around the nerve endings. The leg fatigue, loss of control, and tingling episodes are called *attacks* or *exacerbations*. We will need to continue to monitor your situation closely. Any questions?" *Facts, about myelin sheath, attacks, uncertainty. No, I don't have questions because it's all a big question mark to me.*

"Not now," I answer. I am light-headed, feel drugged. I just want to go home and lie down.

Out the door, I suddenly feel a touch of relief. I look up at the bright, blue sky and beautiful green leaves on the trees, the shimmering green color that says spring is in full bloom. I smile. *It is not a brain tumor, not a brain tumor. Maybe this MS is something I can manage.*

My cane and I make it home and I spend most of the day lying down. Mind over matter. I will keep moving ahead, one day at a time.

I don't call my parents. In fact I tell no one about the diagnosis. I don't want anybody to worry about me and don't want to console them when they hear me say "MS." I don't want to say anything that might jeopardize my job. I can't give my brain a second to consider saying something. It seems best to keep my head down and barrel through it.

CHAPTER 12

SoHo

Two months later, in the fall of 1978, prednisone out of my system, I am walking better. That's a huge contrast from where I was two months ago, wondering if I'd make it across the street in twenty seconds. What I'm learning about this condition is that sometimes I'm symptomatic and sometimes I'm normal.

On a Saturday morning, Melody calls. "Let's get dressed up and go to SoHo tonight," she says.

"Sounds like fun to me," I say. SoHo is not a part of Manhattan I frequent. It's a funky area filled with artists, musicians, and upcoming clothing designers. I'm game to go.

In black, high-heeled leather boots, black pants, silver blouse that shimmers, and flowing black jacket, Melody looks artsy yet sophisticated. Top that with her black turban that she bought from a 1940s clothes shop. She wears a silver, antique bracelet she borrowed from her mother.

I give a lot of thought to my outfit—flared black slacks with thin orange, vertical stripes, a silk Marimekko type of design, loose blouse with a splash of orange and green, and my dressy knee-length black jacket. I feel put together, attractive, which I haven't over the last several months with my cane and slumped shoulders.

As we stroll down Broadway, complimenting ourselves on our evening adventure, a group of two men and a woman, around our age, pass and one of the men says, "Great look!"

"Put your arm around my shoulder and I will grab your waist," Melody says. "Let's see if we can get more people to do a double take when they see us, pass by, and then look back for another glance."

She then turns to me and says, "Hey, so glad you are walking better. Who knew walking down the street could be so much fun!"

Yes, I am walking better right now. Over the last couple of months, I have not needed my cane. Although I stay positive and upbeat on the outside, I talk to myself frequently to calm the chatter in my head that keeps asking, *When will the next attack come?* But no chatter tonight. I am in the moment, enjoying walking down the street with Melody.

◆ ◆ ◆

"Did you see that couple look at us?" she says, obviously loving it. A block away, I see a woman standing provocatively on the corner.

"A hooker?" I ask, knowing she is.

"We are okay when we stick together," Melody assures me. "Anyway, we are almost there and I am famished."

A lanky, blond-haired man, with black leather pants and wide-collar lavender shirt, greets us at the door. "IDs, please."

"Sure," Melody says with her big smile, looking like she is ready to flirt. "I love to be carded."

◆ ◆ ◆

It's been my pattern for months to spend a night a week with Melody, our own kind of adult sleepover. Sometimes we smoke a joint and sometimes not. We hang out in her upper bunk but do not have sex. I wonder what it would be like if this were a real love relationship, not just play time. Neither of us goes there because Melody is involved in an intimate relationship with two people, both of whom I've met. One is a street-smart, slick guy who is mysterious to me. I have no idea what he does, how he earns a living, who his friends are. What makes me nervous is his announcing to both of us that he doubts if he will live to be forty years old.

I express my concerns to Melody, that he is not a good influence, that he is too controlling and he does not seem to respect women as equals. I also think he might be involved with drugs, maybe selling them. She says yes, she knows, but I don't see her backing away.

◆ ◆ ◆

What happens, though, is that *I* begin to back off. I continue in her class, enjoy meals together, but stop staying overnight, stop being around when this slick man is present. He rings an alarm bell for me.

Soon, Melody invites me to a big party on a Saturday night on Third Avenue near 48th Street. It will be in a friend of a friend's apartment with an eclectic group. Having a little trepidation because I may only know one or two people, I suck up my inhibitions and say yes.

At 9:00 p.m. I leave my apartment in my new black pants, long black jacket, and large, gold, hooped earrings and head for the party. I feel like I've captured a little New York style with my outfit. I'm ready for a fun evening. I push the button for apartment 5D and am buzzed in.

"Hi, I'm Arlene, a friend of Melody's," I say to the thirty-something man with slick black hair and a black turtleneck who opens the door. He reminds me of a taller Al Pacino.

"Hi, I'm Mikey," he says, in a strong New York accent. "Come in. Melody is in the living room," he adds, pointing the way to where she is.

I spot her as I enter the huge living room, which has a fully stocked bar, a large black leather sofa, and dark gray suede chairs arranged at either end. The furniture is very modern, lots of steel on table and chair legs. Melody jumps up and gives me a big, heartfelt hug. She looks dazzling in her flowing multicolored caftan and black pants, and her right wrist is covered with four or five plain round bracelets.

The dips, chips, and guacamole sit on a glass table at one end of the living room. I recognize and greet a woman who takes Melody's class with me. The noise increases as more people enter the apartment and conversation intensifies. I meet Melody's policeman friend. He is pleasant enough, buff, and has on a navy flannel shirt, brown leather jacket, and pressed blue jeans.

I go to the bar to get a scotch and water. I notice a couple of men going into the bedroom, closing the door behind them. A few minutes later, a skinny man with thinning blond hair and wire-rimmed glasses comes into the living room carrying a large briefcase, and walks to the back of the room. He places his case on a straight chair by the door and cracks it open, just a bit. I happen to see it's filled with stacks of cash. He closes the case and enters the bedroom.

I feel danger in the air. Something is going on and it is not good. Glancing over to my right, I see the policeman talking, leaning against a wall with beer in hand. He raises his arm to scratch his forehead, exposing a handgun in a holster, strapped around his shoulder and nestled up against his armpit.

◆ ◆ ◆

Oh my, it has to be drugs. Cocaine. That's what people must be doing in the bedroom, smoking or free-basing cocaine. And maybe selling cocaine. If it were marijuana, it would be out in the living room, out in the open. Not so with cocaine. I wonder what the policeman knows.

"Where's Melody?" I ask Mikey, sensing I might want to flee the premises.

"I think she must be in the bedroom," he says nonchalantly. "Do you want me to check?"

"No," I respond, put my glass on the table, stand up, and turn toward the front door. "Just tell her I needed to go home."

With Melody, I have been breaking my personal boundaries, taking more risks, putting myself among people I have little in common with. It's been fun and I don't want to retreat into all my old patterns, but the danger of hard-drug selling is an activity I want no part of. I don't want to see the headline "Aspiring Young Professional Arrested in Drug Deal Gone Bad."

— CHAPTER 13 —

Tight Skin

The next weekend, I'm home thinking about what might be fun to do when Mom and Dad come to visit in a few days. Maybe the musical *Evita* on Broadway, a walk through Central Park, the boat tour that circles Manhattan? The only specific thing they mentioned was visiting the Statue of Liberty and Ellis Island, where Dad landed and began his life in America.

"Don't plan too much," Mom said on the phone last night. "We just want to spend time with you."

I call for the Circle Boat Tour schedule and ask the woman on the other end to repeat the information because I can't hear her very well. *The connection seems okay. What's the deal? Was she talking softly? Is it me?* I have to ask her to repeat the information three times and it seems she's getting annoyed with me.

In my office a couple of hours later, a colleague stops by my desk asking for information about the LaGuardia project. As she talks, I turn my head side to side, testing out each ear. *Something is wrong in my right ear.* Her words are muffled. I ask her to repeat, facing her head-on. My left ear seems fine.

At 30 Park Avenue in the evening, the skin on my head feels tight, like my skull has grown too big for the amount of skin around it. *Is there something swelling up in my head? Should I go to a hospital emergency room?* I call the emergency number Dr. P gave me. I convince myself that it will be okay until tomorrow morning and ask for an appointment first thing in the morning.

The following morning at 8:00, Dr. P examines me and says I need another CT scan. I ask if I should be concerned with the amount of radiation I'm being exposed to, but he doesn't think it is of concern. That's not reassuring, but what choice do I have? He believes this is related to the other symptoms I've been experiencing. Once again, he extends his arm toward me, with a prescription for prednisone in hand. It seems so predictable and I don't like that prednisone is his automatic go-to. The scan results don't point to a specific cause other than there's inflammation that is causing the swelling. The prednisone may take three months to fully work, and part of my hearing will come back, but slowly. Really? That's it? No other explanation? No other treatment? It all feels vague and inconclusive.

The next day, I complete a CT scan. The radiologist and my physicians team say it's neurological. I have 85 percent hearing loss in my right ear. Along with that, my swollen-feeling head seems like it is six inches above the pillow when I lie in bed on my right side. It is so weird not feeling my head sink into the pillow, readying itself for a good night's sleep. It reminds me of when I had no feeling on the bottom of my feet at Dayton's and felt like I was floating above the floor.

◆ ◆ ◆

Three days later, Mom and Dad arrive and I meet them at their hotel in Gramercy Park on 23rd Street. It's a great neighborhood with tree-lined streets and quaint, historical buildings. Their hotel is thirteen blocks from my apartment and they want to walk it. As we walk north, I see Dad wrap his little finger around Mom's little finger as they stroll up the street. Mom looks like autumn in her four-button auburn coat and gold scarf.

I've been taking prednisone for a few days and feel a little bloated. The feeling in my head is still off. I hope Mom and Dad don't suspect anything. I think about saying something, but my desire to have a fun, relaxed time overshadows everything and I stay silent.

I want Mom and Dad to have ice cream at Serendipity on East 60th Street and they are eager to go there. Seated at a small, round table, I slant my chair slightly to the right. I have to rely on my left ear to hear Mom. Dad, in his customary suit and tie, leans his arms on the table and looks at me with a twinkle in his eye.

"Do you remember how much you loved going to the automat on 42nd Street when we were here for the '64 World's Fair?" he asks. "You wanted to eat every meal at Horn and Hardart," he adds, and I know he is bringing it up because he loved it too.

I haven't thought about that in years. I loved the automat, the big restaurant with rows and rows of vending machines that housed full meals. Dad gave us money to go to the cashier, who gave back a little coin that fit in a slot. My eyes widened big as I went back and forth, looking inside the rectangular, well-lit steel-and-glass boxes against the wall, seeing sandwiches, fried chicken, macaroni and cheese, and pie and cake slices. Once I chose, I put my coin in the slot and turned the knob. The glass door clicked. I lifted the door and pulled out my food. It was so much more fun than a cafeteria because in the automat, each piece of food had its own compartment.

I love Dad when he's relaxed and joyfully remembering fun family times. The World's Fair and enjoying New York City stand out in his mind and mine, too. And now I live here. I think Dad's pleased and proud of me. I don't want to say anything to burst his bubble.

After enjoying our ice cream, we walk over to Central Park and stroll up the pathways, seeing beautiful orange and red leaves on the trees, kids playing Frisbee, and even a juggler entertaining the people who seem to just be walking, without a planned destination. Even with my head feeling like it's about twice its normal size, I still can focus on the lovely day and the carefree feeling of walking with no time constraints. Mom says she can see why I like the city so much, particularly with this oasis in the middle of Manhattan that offers trees, wildlife, and calm. Dad puts his arm around my shoulder and says he's glad to see me loving the city and so happy.

Our time together was so ideal during those beautiful October days. I didn't want to bring down the mood by discussing my recent symptoms. I did consider telling them, but it's been nine years of keeping my health issues to myself, so even if I were to say something, I wouldn't know where to start.

CHAPTER 14

Huge Decision

It's the next month in 1979 and images of violence, anger, and protest—yelling, marching, turning cars over—flash across my TV screen. Flashback to Iowa, senior year, campus violence with protests against the Vietnam War—the toxic air, the chaos of people running in all directions. This seems worse. Much worse. Is the world in peril, about to be totally destabilized? Staring at my thirteen-inch TV, I freeze in fear as thousands of Iranians fill the streets, carrying banners with Ayatollah Khomeini's picture. The news shouts at me that Iranian militants have seized the US embassy in Tehran and are holding hostages. What I'm seeing makes my problems at work seem trivial. My continuing hearing loss fades in comparison to this display of hate.

◆ ◆ ◆

I can feel the stress and tension from the television. As an antidote, I ask Lorraine to go with me to Central Park to be with the trees, watch them do their magic, transforming green into gorgeous red, orange, and yellow leaves. I love the fall color extravaganza, the leaves, one by one, detaching from the branches, floating through the air on their way to resting on the earth. Even in such a dense urban environment, nature is evident, reminding me that everything has its season.

I have felt minor symptom relief as a result of the prednisone, but I'm hoping that what's going on with my hearing and the sensation of swelling will be just a temporary season as well and will eventually go away.

◆ ◆ ◆

The next day, I'm sitting at my desk in my doorless office when the phone rings.

"Hello," I say after picking up the beige phone receiver.

"Hi, Arlene. This is Brian. I want this call to be confidential. Are you in a place where you can talk freely?"

I'm not, so I tell Brian, who is the corporate director of human resources at United headquarters in Chicago, that I will find a private office or conference room and call him back.

Does he want me to be on a special task force? I ponder, walking down the long, narrow hallway, then into a small, gray conference room. *He's not a person who would normally call me. What's up?*

I dial the long-distance number and Brian picks up on the first ring. He talks with lots of energy, excited to tell me that a budget has just been approved for a new department at headquarters in Chicago: Human Resource Planning. He strongly urges me to interview for the newly developed manager position. One other person is in the running, but I'm the definite favorite candidate.

Our conversation concludes. Standing up, my legs feel weak. I feel like a balloon just popped in my body, sucking all the air out.

I should feel pleased, happy, affirmed by the compliments from Brian about my work and potential that higher management sees in me. But I don't. I love New York City. I'm making good progress in my job, now a little over three years into it. And I still have hearing loss, am less than one hundred percent of my healthy self. *Return to Chicago? Go back? I don't want to go backward.*

◆ ◆ ◆

I know another opportunity will not come my way if I say no to an interview, say no to an amazing opportunity to build a brand-new department from scratch. Few people have that offered to them in their entire career. Plus, creating structure, content, and meaning to an ambiguous situation excites me. That is what this is about. Creating something out of nothing. After mulling this over, I get back to Brian and tell him I will interview.

But . . . there is no way I can get on an airplane with compromised hearing and the skin on my head still feeling tight. One thing airline employees understand is that flying with an ear problem isn't a good idea. So, I use that to my advantage. I stick to the truth but omit the details and just say I'm having ear problems. I know that if I fully divulge my health issues I will be seen as weak or incapable.

Brian completely understands, quickly making an alternate plan. He will fly to Newark International Airport to interview with me in an airport office.

I'm conflicted as I board the bus on 42nd Street, heading off to Newark. This job is intriguing and maybe a once-in-a-career opportunity. They want me. But I don't feel ready to leave NYC. I'm coming into my own, feeling comfortable as a manager and also personally, opening myself to more expressiveness, more vulnerability, more creativity in my relationships, particularly with Melody.

The evening after the interview, I sit in my apartment contemplating my decision if Brian should offer me the position. My heart is in NYC and I feel I can personally grow here and experience new relationships that will challenge and fulfill me. On the other hand, this new job would be a groundbreaking move for a female manager, especially one as young as I am. I know if I don't take it, I'll never be given a big promotion and it will be career halting.

Brian offers me the position. I take the plunge, say yes. I accept the challenge of creating a new human resources department for United. I wonder what it will be like to move forward in a place I am going back to?

— CHAPTER 15 —

Mixed Feelings

It's mid-January 1980. I'm on a United flight from New York City to Chicago. My ear problem has subsided and the skin on my head is completely normal. I don't think about that now, though, because I'm sad to leave. Even with my physical challenges, I love New York and want to experience so much more of it. When asked what I wanted to do about my apartment at 30 Park Avenue, I said I wanted to take it with me, including my view of the Empire State Building. I want all of NYC to come with me: my job, the philharmonic, my theater-going friends, Lorraine, and Melody, too. After that party a few months ago, Melody and I talked. She apologized and said she treasured our friendship, which we both have worked to build stronger. And now I'm creating distance by leaving.

Inside, I don't want to leave yet. I've been learning so much about myself in NYC. Still with a long way to go, I've learned to ask for help, which I've been reluctant to do all my life. I've learned it's okay to talk about my feelings, okay to be vulnerable. My body has given me no choice but to be vulnerable and shaken.

I'm leaving in the midst of just getting started, but the chance to build a brand-new department does not come along often.

I've tried to keep my body and spirit strong, telling myself it's mind over matter. I can get through anything. But the sentence Melody often repeated continues to echo in my mind: "Your body doesn't lie." As I sit in this plane thirty-five thousand feet in the air, I know there's so much more to learn about being healthy in my mind, my body, and my spirit. I'm not sure what it all means.

I don't want to look at Chicago as going backward. I haven't lived there for three and a half years. The twenty-nine-year-old I was then was not nearly as aware as the person I am now. I want to move toward a new dynamic that creating a new corporate department and living in a new apartment will bring. I'm renting a friend's vacant apartment for three months, but then what? *What if my legs give out? What if I'm not up to the new job, one I will create from scratch?* I'm excited. I'm scared. I'm uncertain about the health of my body. I feel alone.

As I lean my head back on the headrest of my airplane seat and close my eyes, I hear Presbyterian minister Elam Davies's reassuring words from when I was about to move to New York City: "God has opened many doors for you and has gone ahead to prepare the way. It is a time to ask for extra strength."

Like a spray of mist passing before my eyes, I remember wandering into the Fourth Presbyterian Church in the Gold Coast of Chicago four years ago, in 1976. It must have been a directed wandering of sorts. I had grown up attending a small Presbyterian church where I learned acceptance and welcoming of all people, as we are all made in the image of God. I was far away from organized religion during college and began to think that Christianity was a product of human beings' need to believe in some force, something bigger, because life can be so hard and scary.

There I was, walking into Fourth Presbyterian, a beautiful sanctuary that easily held a thousand. I sat in the back on that Sunday morning, wanting to remain anonymous. In the raised pulpit at the front of the sanctuary stood a distinguished-looking man, the preacher, with a strong Welsh accent, leaning over the lectern, talking to the congregation: "God loves you. God accepts you as you are, even with your unbelief." He said it was okay to have questions and doubts. I had a lot of them. He, a person who was *supposed* to have all the answers, was admitting to everyone that he had doubts too. That was appealing and drew me in to listen.

I sat up straight in the wooden pew, feeling his words come directly toward me. He was talking to me. I felt like I was the only person in the room.

The next day after that Sunday morning experience at Fourth Church, I picked up the phone and called Dr. Davies's office seeking an appointment to see him. The woman on the other end of the phone asked what I wanted to see him about. Not being articulate, I said my wish was to ask him what Christianity is really about and what it means when he says we have to make a decision, a choice about who and what we worship.

I did get an appointment, discovering he looked smaller in person, close up, than he did in the pulpit with his flowing robe. He had short, gray hair and looked like a professor, smart and intellectual. He was filled with compassion and wisdom. Our conversations continued every three to four months and I freely asked him not only spiritual and religious questions but also for advice on business and family issues. While living in New York City, I called Dr.

Davies and shared my scary physical problems with him, sought his advice and reassurance.

Now, on my way back to Chicago, I hope we might resume some regular in-person conversations about faith and life's big questions.

The captain announces, "Ladies and gentlemen, I am turning the seat belt sign on. Return to your seats and fasten your seat belts. We are starting our descent into Chicago."

CHAPTER 16

A Competitive Edge

W hat a contrast. This is my first week on the job with a frenzied pace in the midst of a gray, sterile environment. As I walk to my second-floor office, all I see is gray: a sea of gray metal desks, gray cubicles surrounded by gray partitions, and gray, speckled linoleum floor. All these cubicles and the offices that line the perimeter announce the pecking order, who has authority and power and who does not. This is United's corporate headquarters, in a Chicago suburb twenty-six miles from the apartment I'm renting. It's February 1980.

My boss, Brian, tells me there are two or three people I need to get rid of because they're not carrying their weight. He said big changes are coming that will likely cause us to have to fire, hire, and furlough people at the same time.

The stakes are high. United struggles with issues unleashed by deregulation of the airline industry two years prior. With that shift, airlines no longer need approval to move in and out of routes. It's a marketplace free-for-all. Competition is stiff. The company is spending over a million dollars to create my new department, Human Resource Planning. Our charge is to help department heads select smart, skilled executives, directors, and managers who will be great forward-looking decision-makers who can help the airline deliver excellent customer service while achieving profitability. We need to have a competitive edge.

For me that means nonstop meetings, planning, strategizing, and adjusting budget projections. I want to show I can be successful in a male-dominated industry. I want to instill excellence in my employees and show my superiors that we will lead the airline industry with the best people.

◆ ◆ ◆

On weekends I start to look at condos, excited to buy my first home. Mom and Dad raised me to work hard, save money, and think through how I spend it. Owning a condo says *I'm here making an investment in my future.* Although I'm new in my job, I feel like I've arrived at a point to make a career here, not just have a job. I start a whirlwind of looking at twenty-two condos in ten days, in Lincoln Park and the Gold Coast.

It's the tour of my twenty-third condo that resonates with me, on Lake Shore Drive, six blocks north of the John Hancock building. As my agent and I walk into the one-bedroom apartment, bright sunshine streams in through large living room windows. My mouth drops open as I gaze at a panoramic view of Lake Michigan out those windows, as far as my eye can see. Sailboats, walkers, bicyclists, a sandy beach are part of the front yard. The expansiveness of the water, the sky, and all the activity outside the window reflect what I feel inside—openness and endless possibilities are in store for me.

"I want to live here!" I exclaim.

I have no doubt that I have found my new home, and here I am, a woman pushing through gender roles, spending the biggest amount of money I can imagine, to purchase a condo. I only experience one iffy moment in the buying process, and it is a big one. When I arrive at the approval point for a loan, the current rate is 16.5 percent! *Can I swing this? Should I?* The answer is "barely," but I forge ahead. At closing time I luck out, slightly, and secure my loan at 12.5 percent. *With this financial stretch, I have to be successful. I must make a good salary and keep my job to be able to pay this mortgage.*

◆ ◆ ◆

Fourth of July weekend 1980. It's move-in time! I feel extra excitement because Melody is coming to Chicago for the weekend. Bobby will join us, and my new friend, Peter. We will have a party and I don't care about not having much furniture, so we will be sitting on the living room floor.

I feel grown-up, a homeowner, with a big new job and great friends to help me celebrate it all. I cannot think of a better way to start a new decade.

Melody arrives with a floppy hat and slicked-back hair, looking like she might be one of Tony's friends in *Saturday Night Fever*. We embrace tightly.

"Oh, my friend, I miss you," Melody says, as if no time has passed.

"Me too. I'm so glad you're here to celebrate my new home," I respond.

After a quick lunch we walk in the underground tunnel out to Lake Michigan, head up the walking trail to Lincoln Park. My friends Carla and Russ meet us there. We want to do a photo shoot. Russ pulls out his camera.

"Let's act like we're movie stars, maybe Judy Garland or Lana Turner," Melody says. "We'll schmaltz it up." Snap, snap, snap, the camera shoots us in front of big rocks, leaning against a large tree, on the sand by the lake. We laugh, imagining ourselves in a movie scene or part of a *Vogue* magazine layout.

We take our shoes off, run across the beach to dip our toes into the water. More pictures.

"I feel like I'm on the French Riviera," Melody says, "far away from the city, from anything I know. I love it."

I do too. Once again, Melody touches the carefree, playful part of me. She brings color, vibrancy, and lightness to my life. I completely forget about my new job in that gray, sterile environment.

CHAPTER 17

A Time to Listen

Four months pass and I hire two industrial psychologists, two clinical psychologists, and three information technology analysts. I continue to get pressure to get rid of Laurie, an employee who has been with the company for thirty-five years, my department's secretary. Laurie is a legend. Everybody knows her.

She is tall and very skinny with wavy, dark brown hair that rests on her shoulders. She has a distinctive walk, stilted, uneven, like she might have stiff or sore joints. Laurie is pleasant, and although it's not her style to start a conversation, she is very willing to engage in one when someone else starts.

"Laurie is slowing down, more and more," Brian had told me early on. "I am not sure she will make it in your new organization."

"Is there a reason Laurie has become ineffective?" I asked.

"Not that I know of," Brian said. "We just think the faster pace, the heavier workload, and more complex tasks are overwhelming her."

There is a pattern here that I have seen repeatedly as I have assumed managerial positions. My superiors quickly point out performance problems and identify people who they think need to be transferred or let go, but they have not done anything about it. There's been no specific conversations with the employees, no paper trail. So far, my male bosses seem to be risk-averse when it comes to dealing with employee performance issues.

I gear up to have a conversation with Laurie, writing out questions to ask her, points I want to cover. I need to be straightforward in telling her that her performance is below expectations and I want to hear her side of the story.

I meet with Laurie in the small conference room near my office and start by affirming her long-term contribution. Then I mention that I know she is having some difficulty with her typing, with her timeliness. I ask if there is something she is dealing with that is affecting her performance.

"Wow, thanks for asking, Arlene," she says, wiping her head with the back of her hand. "I've been diagnosed with Parkinson's disease. I am challenged every day to keep up," she adds, smiling as if a lead weight has been lifted from her chest.

She continues with a comment I find astounding: "Nobody has ever asked me if something is wrong. I just didn't say anything, feeling afraid that I would lose my job." She stands up, walks over to me, bends down, and gives me a hug.

I'm the first one to ask her if something is wrong? Is a chronic condition seen as a weakness regardless of performance level? I am in that category, although nobody at work knows. I quickly compartmentalize and put that in the back of my mind. Otherwise, I might worry and spend time wondering *what if.* I've learned from colleagues here that part of the fear factor with employees is that with a preexisting condition, getting insurance coverage is next to impossible. If they lose their job, they lose their insurance. Fortunately, I'm good at compartmentalizing, knowing it's mind over matter that propels me forward.

Laurie is so relieved to have her situation revealed. She smiles more, becomes more outgoing. This is a situation that calls for justice and fairness. My core value of treating people fairly, taking action to do what's right, comes into play here. I changed the unfair judicial system at the University of Iowa from the inside out, took the position in Minneapolis to work on fair policies and treatment of employees, learned to take action from the protest days in Iowa. I work diligently to get her unused vacation bridged to retirement in good standing. It takes six months, but it is well worth it because she leaves with her pension and medical benefits that are essential to her well-being.

— CHAPTER 18 —

Dad Talks to Me

O n a sunny, pleasant late-spring Saturday, I pack my little overnight bag, climb into my maroon Chevy Nova,
and head out to Mendota for a weekend visit with Mom
and Dad. I rewind the conversation I had with Laurie, seeing her
transformation from extreme nervousness at the beginning of our
meeting to elation at the end. I wonder if she thought I was calling
her in to fire her. I wonder why no one had taken the time to ask
her a simple, straightforward question about why she seemed to be
struggling. I feel good about this positive outcome, for Laurie and
for me, modeling a professional yet caring approach to a complex
employee-performance situation.

Reaching Route 30, I take the exit ramp so I can go through the
small towns of Hinckley and Waterman. Dark, rich soil dots the
landscape along with typical two-story wooden farmhouses and red
barns, reminding me of my Midwest childhood and the prosperity

we enjoyed because of those farmers' care and love for their corn and their soybeans. I see the Mendota sign, *Home of the Sweet Corn Festival*, and then the Del Monte plant on the east side of town.

On Saturday evening Mom, Dad, and I venture to a childhood favorite Italian restaurant in LaSalle, about fifteen miles south of Mendota, for fried chicken and a side order of spaghetti. I tell them about Laurie, how great my new condo is, already having friends over for dinner parties, and how much I'm enjoying worship services and my volunteer work at Fourth Church. Mom, particularly, is always asking about my friends.

On Sunday morning, Dad completes his rounds at the hospital as he has for decades and makes a house call out in the country a couple of miles north of town. I'm in my childhood bedroom going through some of my mementos in my closet: dolls and stamp and rock collections. Mom wants me to start sorting through things to decide what I want to keep and what I want to give or throw away. Around noon, I smell the familiar and aromatic fried chicken that Mom still makes in her gold, electric fry pan. I walk out of the bedroom, through the living room into the den. Dad is sitting in his comfortable chair, leaning forward, looking at some papers he has sitting on the ottoman. He looks up at me, removing his round, wire-rim glasses from his face.

"Are you dating someone?" he asks, plunging right in. I freeze in place, shocked that he asks this out of the blue.

"No, not at the moment," I respond, continuing to stand while facing him seated in his chair.

"You only talk about your friends. Friends are great and being self-sufficient is great, but family is everything," he says, focusing his gaze directly on mine. "You should not only think about your career and travels but also about your personal future, about getting married and having children," he adds as he picks up some of his papers and stands up. "I'm hungry. Let's go have some lunch," he says, as if eating chicken is a natural transition from a statement about marriage and children.

He really does not want to hear from me, nor have a dialogue on this subject. I receive his words as a monologue, as something he strongly believes and wants to impart to his youngest daughter. He does not raise his voice but is very clear about wanting me to think about a future that includes marriage. What can I say to that when a response is not asked for? Nothing.

I think back to high school. In my junior year, I looked at being an American Field Service (AFS) student, living abroad with a family for a year. Mom was very enthusiastic and supportive. Dad said okay. Although there was no guarantee about location, I chose England, Ireland, France, Germany, and Italy as my top picks.

Early steps completed, the next was a personal interview. Representatives were scheduled to drive to our home to talk with me and my parents. Two weeks before the interviews, I was in the beige stuffed chair in the den reading *The Red and the Black* by Stendhal. Dad, still in his shirt and tie, walked in.

"I want to talk with you about the AFS program," he calmly said, but in a serious tone, which was not unusual for him. "After dinner."

"Okay," I said, glancing up to acknowledge him. I didn't give it a second thought.

After dinner was over, I helped Mom clear the table and dry the dishes after she washed and rinsed them. My brother was at basketball practice. I went to my room to get my books together for class in the morning. Although the door was open, I heard a knock.

"Can I come in?" Dad asked as he walked in the room, closing the door behind him.

"Sure." I sat down on my bed, facing Dad, who sat down in my desk chair.

"About this AFS program, I really didn't think it would go this far." His eyes winced, zeroing straight into my gaze. I sat motionless, at attention.

My neck muscles turned to rock. My breathing sped up. My head started to spin. I froze.

"This will make your mother sick, having you so far away. She'll worry. She'll never say that to you, but I will." *I don't believe this. Mom is excited for me. He's the one who doesn't want me to leave. It's Dad.* The reasons for his saying this came to light years later after discovering more about his family. Dad left Europe and his family to come to the United States, and many in his family died in the Holocaust.

I looked at him. With my dry throat, I had trouble getting words out, but I said, "Mom is so supportive. She has been encouraging me to do this all along. This is an opportunity of a lifetime."

"You're being selfish. I want you to cancel the interviews. I don't want you to go." He didn't wait for me to say anything, just got up and walked out of the room.

My entire body shook, worse than shivering from extreme cold. I stretched my leg out to stand on the floor, but it refused to hold me, and I started to fall but caught myself by grabbing on to the edge of the bedpost. Slowly, I got my balance, walked down the hall to the bathroom, and washed my face with cold water. *What just happened? What do I do?* I went to the phone and called a good friend to go over to her house and vent.

What happened from there? I fibbed and told Mom that as the interview neared, the thought of living in another country for a year was losing appeal. Living so far away for an entire year would just be too long. I didn't say a word to Mom about what Dad said to me. I was concerned she would worry much more about Dad making me cancel the interview than worry about my living in a foreign country for a year. She would worry about my dreams being dashed. I would worry that if I pushed ahead and left home, Dad might take out his frustrations on Mom. I canceled the interview. Not one more word was ever said about AFS.

♦ ♦ ♦

Now after the marriage and kids talk, it occurred to me that I didn't share with Dad my recurring episodes with pain and numbness so that he could better understand me. I could not make it clear to him that marriage and family *were* important but my MS diagnosis created a barrier to those objectives. It was not all him. It was me, too.

After the weekend visit, I wake up the next morning thinking about my father's question, about his comments that I should seriously think about marrying at some point. He caught me off guard. I stood motionless and listened. Actually, I think that's exactly what he wanted me to do. He did cause me to ask myself questions. *Do I want marriage? Why have I backed off relationships when they get too close?* I have no answers at the moment and put this subject in the back of my mind.

As I sit up and put my right leg on the floor to stand up, it feels weak. My ankle twitches.

Oh no, this is way too familiar. . . .

– CHAPTER 19 –

Confiding

The weakness in my ankle dissipates quickly and I race through the week spending twelve-hour days in the office. My stamina remains strong, as do my legs and ankles.

The following Saturday, I am walking three blocks from my condo, headed to the grocery store. Suddenly I stop and stand motionless in the middle of the sidewalk. A warm sensation fills the seat of my pants. *Oh no. I've had an accident with no warning. Nothing told me I needed to find a bathroom.* My body stiffens, feels wooden. I turn 180 degrees, walk gingerly back to my condo, take my pants off, and throw them into the wash. I see that I just had a major bowel movement walking down the sidewalk.

I feel limp and confused about what just happened. My stomach wasn't upset and I didn't have cramps. *How did this just happen without me knowing it beforehand? Why didn't my body tell me?*

The next day, at home while walking into my kitchen, the back part of my upper left leg feels like it's wet. Rubbing my leg with my hand, it isn't wet. How strange; the wet feeling isn't real. This is alarming. My nerve sensors that signal the need for a toilet and that signal wetness on my skin aren't working. *I can't live with this.*

I take Monday off from work to see my neurologist. He tells me these symptoms are common with MS. He writes out a prescription for medication to help moderate my symptoms. It may take two to three days before I feel any effect and then I will hopefully feel when I need to go to the bathroom. The "hopefully" is a bit disconcerting, although I know he can't guarantee one-hundred-percent effectiveness. How will I manage leaving my condo if I can't get this under control quickly?

These incidents are embarrassing and hard to talk about, even with a doctor. Along with my episodes of weak legs and hearing loss, will this new uncertainty become an ongoing part of my life? My spirit sinks. I need to talk with Peter.

Peter, whom I met through Bobby, has become a good friend. I met Peter when I lived in New York City and he lived in Chicago. He's slender and wears fashionable round, rimless glasses. A partner in a commercial interior design firm, he has a wonderful eye for design, proportion, and space. I rely on him for hanging my art, picking out furniture, and selecting paint colors.

Our relationship is comfortable and authentic. We talk about everything, from apartment decorating to family issues, work, health. Peter is open and willing to listen to every detail I want to lay out about the anxiety I live with regarding new, unexpected physical symptoms. I tell him about the incident on the sidewalk when my colon emptied before I was aware. He gets that it's embarrassing and says so. I feel no judgment, just caring for me and how I feel.

Although Peter is in a relationship with Kevin, we do a lot together, particularly going to movies, out to dinner, and to the ballet. We recently saw the American Ballet Theatre, or ABT, at the Civic Opera House, a magnificent performance space. Even outside of performances, I visualize the ABT dancers, graceful as swans, light on their feet. That picture helps me relax and feel like time is suspended. Peter and I talk about ballet, and in those times when I have anxiety about my physical uncertainty, it's natural for our conversation to move into the gracefulness of dancers.

I call my sister and brother, just to let them know about my new symptoms and the specific incident while walking to the grocery store. Carol expresses concern and compassion.

"Do you have confidence in your doctor?" she asks. "I'm sorry you are going through so much uncertainty. Be sure to let me know how I can help."

David is supportive too, and with his experience as a gastroenterologist, he wants to know what medicine the neurologist prescribed. "It should help without any side effects," he says. "I know the doctor and he is an expert in his field, so hopefully that gives you confidence in him."

"It does and it helps to have you confirm that," I say.

"Okay, let me know if there is anything I can do," he adds.

◆ ◆ ◆

I also confide in Dr. Davies. I make an appointment to see him. As I walk into his office, he opens his arms wide and gives me a big hug.

"So good to see you, Arlene. It's been two or three months since we've talked. How's your health?" Dr. Davies says in his familiar lilting accent. As always, he's smartly dressed in a dark gray suit, black tie, and polished black shoes.

"I'm generally not a worrier, but I'm on edge," I respond. "Recently I had new symptoms, misfires with the mechanism that tells me I need to go to the bathroom. It's embarrassing. That gives me ongoing anxiety about what's coming next that will throw me off my game."

"I'm not surprised," Dr. Davies says, "especially since you're not one-hundred-percent sure of what you're dealing with."

I switch subjects and tell him about my father wanting me to get married and my silent reaction, how I've thought about that and my sexual identity, how it doesn't seem to be a big deal to me whether my attractions are to a man or a woman. Feeling like I'm rambling with my thoughts, I stop.

"Questions and doubts are okay, Arlene," Dr. Davies says, rolling his tongue over the *r* in my name. "It's challenging to learn to accept things as they are, whatever the limitations. God is not causing this, giving you limitations to show you there's something greater. What God does is help us take our limitations and continually work with them for good purposes."

The next words Dr. Davies says about relationships are profound, and I ask him if it's okay if I write them down. He says yes, so pen on paper I write, *Remember that God accepts us with all our complexities and loves us unconditionally. I encourage you to keep searching, keep open to new relationships that may be fulfilling, without trying to put expectations on what they might look like.*

As we close our conversation, Dr. Davies congratulates me on being elected to serve on the major governing body of Fourth Church. In April, two weeks from now, I will be among several church leaders being ordained and installed during a Sunday morning worship service for a six-year term on the Session.

This is a big deal. I call Mom to see if she and maybe Dad can join me for this important event. Mom says she doubts if Dad can come because he has a couple of critically ill patients in the hospital. She would love to come but isn't sure if she can. She doesn't want to leave Dad alone on a Sunday afternoon when they both work on completing insurance forms for patients.

The Tuesday after my installation, I receive a message at work that my brother called and wants to talk to me at 11:00 a.m. *A call at work, really? That never happens.* As I sit alone in a gray conference room waiting for the call, my heart beats quickly and I start to perspire. The phone rings.

In my brother's normal formal tone, he says, "This is your brother, Arlene. Bad news. Dad suffered a massive heart attack this morning and died."

— CHAPTER 20 —

Discoveries

Standing in the large funeral home room, I feel clammy, with a dry throat. It's hard to swallow. I stand, stare around the room, and notice men and women mingling and talking quietly, but I'm not focusing on any one person. Everyone looks just slightly out of focus. It's the last Saturday in April 1983.

"Okay. It is time to form a small line," Mom says, walking toward me. I admire her stamina, her strength, which I definitely do not feel at the moment. In her black cotton dress and black pumps, she exhibits good posture, with a serious look on her face. Her eyes are bright and alert. Although she clasps a single Kleenex in her right hand, she doesn't look like she is on the verge of tears. She is very composed.

It is Mom, then Carol, David, and me. We form a small receiving line, readying ourselves for people to stop and pay their respects to Dad. My knees feel weak. In my black blazer and black skirt, I'm glad I have on flat shoes with my black nylons, since I know we might be standing for quite a while. I take a deep breath, then sigh. I remind myself to keep breathing. I'm sad, shocked about Dad's sudden death. My legs feel okay, but what if they weaken, if I can't stand? The medicine has been working to allow my body to signal when I need to find a bathroom. What if it fails when I'm around so many people? I stand in the midst of my secrets I didn't tell Dad or Mom and certainly wouldn't tell anybody else who has come to pay their respects. My sister and brother are the only ones here in whom I have confided. If I need help, I can rely on them.

I told Mom, before we left the house, that I did not want to look at Dad lying in the open casket. I want to remember him as vital and alive, not motionless. I was nervous about saying that to her, thinking it might be disrespectful.

"Arlene," she said, putting her hand on my shoulder, "that's just fine. I understand and it's okay."

The women and men in the room see us forming a line, so one by one, they come forward to greet us, starting with Mom. I glimpse at her out of the corner of my eye. She extends her hand. She extends her arms to receive hugs. "Thank you, thanks for coming," I hear her say.

After greeting Mom, each individual greets Carol, then David, then me. One by one, people shake my hand and share their individual stories:

"I'm so sorry, Arlene. I'm Joe," the short, dark-haired, middle-aged man says to me. "Your dad meant everything to our family. He was always available, would fit us into his schedule, even when it was full. What a marvelous doctor. . . ."

"Your dad delivered my three babies. . . ."

"Sorry for your family. Your father has been our doctor for over thirty years. We will miss him terribly. . . ."

"So sorry for your loss. Your dad saved my life. I was caught under a combine when I was twelve."

"I am sorry. What a lovely family you are, and your dad meant more than I can say. He listened. He took time. He was brilliant, the best doctor ever. . . ."

"I'm sorry for you. Your dad was great to the hospital staff. He was a terrific doctor and had a good sense of humor. We always liked seeing him come in for rounds. We will really miss him."

"So sorry, Arlene. Our family depended on your father's expertise and kind care. He was very special. . . ."

My throat is dryer. My back aches from standing in one place for over an hour. People keep coming, some I know, others complete strangers.

I walk over to the rectangular table with the guest book and pitcher of water. I pour a glass of water and sit down. My mind flashes back thirty years—getting into the car in our garage, about to take off for Wisconsin Dells. Dad was on the phone inside in the den. We couldn't go right now, he told us, because he was needed in the hospital. In all the trips planned for Wisconsin, I never knew if we would be late in taking off or not go at all. Dad's patients were the priority.

After all, Dad was really quite remarkable. I knew he came to the United States after graduating from medical school in Paris. He had $500 and didn't speak English. He was proud of his family and his medical practice that he built from nothing.

For the first time, today, I understand, hearing all the people from Mendota, LaMoille, Compton, and the farms in between who needed Dad, who counted on him. They loved him.

Yet I wish some of his family could be here to witness this memorial to him, but none of them are in the greeting line. They all live in Europe. In fact, there is a bit of mystery surrounding where Dad came from. For today, though, I'm glad to know he is remembered so fondly. I am grateful for him.

CHAPTER 21

Asking Mom Questions

Home for the weekend for Dad's funeral, Mom, Carol, David, and I honor Dad's life and reminisce about our trips as a family to Wisconsin Dells, taking a train to Seattle for the 1962 World's Fair, visiting Mom's brother on a farm in south central Illinois, going to New Salem to visit Abraham Lincoln sites.

Memories. As we sit around the kitchen table remembering the good times, it hits me that Dad never talked about being young, what he and his family did for fun. In fact, I don't remember him talking about his early life at all. What I know is that, in recent years, he and Mom have visited his two brothers, Joseph in Belgium and Kola in France. I met Joseph and his wife when they visited us and later when I stayed with them in Liege, Belgium, for a few days while in college.

I have questions about Dad's background that he never talked about. What about the passport I saw on his desk a few years ago that said he was from Lodz, Poland, when he always said he was from

Liege, Belgium? Why was his brothers' last name Falkowski and he changed his to Faulk after he arrived in the United States? Carol, David, and I once overheard that Dad's father might have been Jewish. If that's true, I wonder what his family might have endured. An impulse hit me as we were reminiscing.

"Mom, did Dad's family hide Jews during World War II or was his family Jewish?" popped out of my mouth.

"Honey, your dad and his family were Jewish."

I was stunned to hear that straightforward comment come out of Mom's mouth. That part of not only his history but also his identity was not ever mentioned in my presence while he was alive. Why? Did he have survivor's guilt? Or was it just too painful? Maybe he didn't share for the same reason I haven't told any people about my MS. I'm afraid they will worry and be fearful for me.

I want to know more, but just like that, Mom says we need to get lunch ready.

– CHAPTER 22 –

Slow Drip

F ive years pass quickly with intensity at work continuing non-stop. It's 1988 and the pattern of hiring, firing, and furloughing employees at the same time continues. My department is in the middle of it all. On the home front, watching the sun rise over Lake Michigan out my front windows never disappoints. The orange sphere moving upward over the horizon starts my days with calm and hope. I love my condo and Chicago. Peter and I continue to frequent the movie theaters and support ballet and live theater. I've developed friendships with women I've met at Fourth Church, and we share stories about being women in business, go out to dinner, and play bridge. I regularly talk with Dena and we rendezvous once a year with five other college friends, the Heavenly Seven, as we're known. My social life is active with good friends, but not with any romantic interest.

My health is stable with no flare-ups over the past five years. My legs are strong and I'm not on any medications. At this point, no thought about when the next symptom will appear enters my mind. It's shoved to the background.

My work travel focuses mainly on two places I love, New York City and San Francisco, where I spend time with Kathie. Travel continues to be a love and reality, across the United States and in Europe. I take the opportunity to vacation in Evian, France, and Geneva, Switzerland, with its breathtaking mountains and pristine air.

Mom continues to live in Mendota, plays bridge, is active volunteering in her church, and travels to great places like Australia, Rome, and Vienna with her friends. We sign up together for a live theater series. She takes the train into Chicago on Sundays, we have lunch, see a wonderful musical, and then she's off on the train to return home in the evening.

◆ ◆ ◆

Things are going smoothly until one chilly day in March. My workday starts with my staff at our regular weekly meeting.

"Morale is so low," one of my managers says. "We hear negative talk all the time." I hear him but turn my focus to my aching right leg. I try to subtly rub it, then get up and walk around the table.

"Leg cramp," I say, but it isn't. It's the problem with my nervous system out of whack. Feeling normal, then not. I have learned to know the signals, the patterns with my body. This isn't good. It's intense and came on suddenly.

◆ ◆ ◆

The next day, after a big staff meeting, I'm home walking from my bedroom into the living room. *Ring. Ring.* I round the corner to my kitchen and pick up the receiver from the wall phone. It's my brother. He asks how I'm doing.

"Okay, I guess. I'm experiencing weakness and have started to limp a bit. I have an appointment with my neurologist next week." David is sorry I'm having a problem and agrees that I should see the neurologist. I discuss my medical issues with him, wanting both his reassurance and recommendations. As a practicing gastroenterologist, he understands much more than I do about medicine and he wants the best for me.

"This might make you feel better," David adds, in an upbeat voice. "Mom's birthday is in two weeks. I've invited her to come to Chicago for a fun birthday dinner at Monique's French restaurant, one of my favorites, as you know. I hope you can come."

"That sounds great," I say. "I'll plan on it."

◆ ◆ ◆

My neurologist, Dr. D, is a physician, a researcher, and the head of a major MS department in a large Chicago hospital complex. He's well respected by his peers, and his passion is research. I make an appointment to see him.

We start in his office, where he sits behind a huge desk opposite me. Books are everywhere—stacked on tables and his desk and filling shelves behind him. He looks like he might be in his early fifties, with tanned skin and perfectly coiffed silver hair. That and his blue shirt and striped tie make him look like he belongs in a *GQ*-type magazine for medical doctors. I tell him about my symptoms; my right leg and foot are getting weaker. My whole body feels weak and limp. He doesn't look directly into my eyes but seems to look at my forehead, then looks down as he takes notes. He seems cold with no bedside manner. But I'm going to stick with him because he's touted as the best in the MS field.

He recommends I enter the hospital for a five-day adrenocorticotropic hormone (ACTH) intravenous treatment, to halt the progression of inflammation. He wants to take aggressive action and wants me in the hospital next week.

"I don't think I can. We're having a big birthday dinner for my mother next week," I tell him. "I want to be there."

With no emotion, he says, "You need to do this as soon as possible so more damage isn't inflicted on your body." He doesn't acknowledge that I made a statement.

What to do? At home that evening, I pour a glass of Chardonnay and sit on my couch. *What choice do I have? I don't think I really have a choice. I'll go into the hospital.*

I make arrangements at work to take some vacation time so I don't have to explain what the real story is. I call David to explain the situation. He thinks I'm making the right decision to have the treatment right away. I add that I don't want him to tell Mom. I'll call her and say I can't come, but I'm not going to tell her that I'm going to the hospital. I've not said anything about my neurological problems over the years, so now it's overwhelming to think how I might explain it all.

On Sunday evening around 5:00, a friend drives me over to Presbyterian/St. Luke's Hospital, just southwest of downtown. I sit very still in the front passenger seat of her car. *This is something I have to do. I hope it works.*

After checking in, I get my plastic bracelet and find the hospital room. It is small, not well lighted, with a bed, side chair, small closet, and bathroom. It is a private room and has a window that looks out over the expressway. I sit on the edge of the bed. My friend gives me a hug and leaves. The treatment starts at 8:00 p.m. and goes through the night. Other than taking my vitals and checking off items I want to eat for my meals the next two days, I have nothing to do.

The next morning I call Mom. I explain that I'm not feeling well, maybe have a cold coming on. Then I tell her I feel terrible about this, but I won't be able to come to her birthday dinner in Chicago. My hands shake. I wonder if she suspects something is wrong. I hang up the phone. I sigh, feel sad, wishing Mom were here with me right now.

– CHAPTER 23 –

Reflecting

It's day three in the hospital and I've been through three overnight treatments of a solution dripping ever so slowly into my body. It's the day of Mom's birthday dinner. I bet they are already at the restaurant. How I wish I could be there. I imagine them at a table with a white tablecloth, fine French dinnerware, and glassware arranged perfectly. Part of the kitchen to the dining room is exposed, revealing shiny copper pans hanging from hooks on the wall. Shelves inlaid on the wall hold scores of wine bottles, French wine that the waiters help pair up with the entrée that is ordered. The room says *bistro* the minute you walk in the front door. I bet Mom is ordering white fish or maybe sole if they have it tonight. David is ordering salmon with a side of the ratatouille he likes so much. If I was there, I would order chicken cordon bleu with frites. My mouth waters thinking about it.

My mind drifts to thinking about Mom. I want to be with her, but the choice I made continues to keep the secret I've had for so many years. I put myself in a bind and I'm the only one to blame.

Mom is so supportive and kind. She would understand and prop me up. But I haven't been able to say anything to her.

I'm concerned that Mom would worry about me. She doesn't show it on the outside—cool, calm, and steady as she is. She keeps her worry on the inside and it's caused her some serious problems over the years. She's had ulcers and was hospitalized twice that I know of for severe ulcers, and I don't want her to develop another one on account of my health issues. I don't think I contributed to these ulcers, nor did Carol, nor did David. Maybe we did a tiny bit just by being kids. No, I think Dad, at least in part, contributed to her worry, her keeping stuff that bothered her inside. Dad could laugh, be a wonderful conversationalist, and be an excellent problem-solver. He also could be unpredictable, moody, and lash out in anger, mostly at Mom, which I thought was totally uncalled for.

◆ ◆ ◆

The worst was when one of us was sick. Dad cared greatly but couldn't emotionally handle it. He was so calm and reasoned with his patients, which I heard from so many people after he died. Not so with us. I remember what it was like in Iowa City, eighteen years ago, when I was in the hospital for tests and asked him to leave my hospital room. Maybe he showed restlessness and anxiety because he couldn't find a resolution, a definite path forward for me.

◆ ◆ ◆

Alone in my hospital room, my mind drifts to imagining what it might have been like if I had been open about my condition. In my mind, I imagine Mom and Dad sitting at their kitchen table, Mom plating up Swiss steak, gravy, mashed potatoes, and green beans.

Dad has had a tough day, dealing with a critically ill patient in the hospital, a woman who has persistent pain and dizziness and it is not clear what the problem is. Silent, Dad sits in his chair waiting for his food.

The scene in my head continues as Dad suddenly breaks his silence, in a raised voice, talking quickly, and says, "I want Arlene to go to Mayo. I want more tests, the best doctors. We have to get a handle on her situation." He fidgets, puts down his fork, gets up from his chair, and paces. He walks out of the kitchen into the den, comes back, and sits back down. He stares ahead, not focusing on Mom or anything else in the room, because he is deep inside his own thoughts. He is trying hard to figure out how to solve a problem, make progress, just as he has done over so many years with his own patients. His persistence and desire to help me get better are real. I know he wants the best for me, for Mom, for all of us. He cares so much it makes him emotional.

A siren outside in the street beyond my window brings my attention back to the present in the hospital room. I start to question myself as I think about all this, hooked up to the drip. Dad's been gone for almost five years. *What am I doing? Why have I continued to do this alone? Might things have been better if I'd said something?*

— CHAPTER 24 —

Relief

I t's two days after Mom's birthday dinner.

I'm momentarily blinded by the bright sunshine in my eyes. The crisp, cool March air feels so refreshing on my skin after being cooped up in a hot, dry hospital room for five days. How great to be out of the hospital, but my footing is unsteady and I feel weak from lack of exercise. Why does it seem that muscles lose strength and tone so much faster than it takes to build them up?

I'm home now and need to focus. I have to get myself strong enough to drive to work, sit through meetings, and have a clear enough head to problem-solve and make decisions.

I toss and turn in bed that evening. My eyelids are heavy and I feel weary but can't sleep. I sit up in bed, grab the glass of water from my nightstand. The nurse told me sleep could be a problem for a while with all the powerful steroids that dripped into me. But it's more than that. My mind is racing and I can even hear my heart beating. I picture Mom in my mind, seeing her smile, feeling her acceptance, her willingness to always listen to me. This secret I have been keeping is driving me crazy. I have to tell her. But what do I tell her? How do I put eighteen years into one conversation?

◆ ◆ ◆

The next morning I'm sitting on my living room couch, still ruminating. I get up, walk to the window, and stare out at Lake Michigan. How calm the blue water is today. My focus comes back to the room. *Okay, whatever comes out of my mouth just does. Arlene, do it now. Go to the phone.*

Slowly I walk from the living room into the kitchen, pick up the phone, sit on my wicker chair in front of my butcher block table, and dial the familiar number.

"Hello," Mom says after three rings. I take a deep breath.

"Hi, Mom. It's Arlene," I respond, in a softer than usual voice. I pause, trying to quickly muster some courage.

"Hi, honey. We missed you at my birthday dinner," she says.

"Oh, Mom, I so wanted to be with you. I need to confess something that I've been holding in for a long time. I'm not sure where to start and I so want you to know how much I need your support."

"Slow down a bit, Arlene. Take your time." I'm sure she is sensing my anxiety as I speak quickly, like a cassette tape in fast forward.

"Remember all those neurological tests in Iowa City, Mom?" I ask, knowing full well she does.

"I sure do," she answers. "That was a long time ago, but I remember it well. You were young, Arlene, just twenty-two." I imagine her visualizing the hospital room, the neurologist, the lack of any conclusion.

"I know I've not said anything," I say, trying to get my racing thoughts to slow down. "Over the years I've continued to have some problems, though nothing as dramatic as losing all feeling from my waist down. It's been weakness in my legs, tingling in my hands and fingers. I've seen neurologists and have taken all kinds of tests. After all those years, I still don't have a definitive diagnosis. In New York City the doctors said they were ninety percent sure it was multiple sclerosis. They, and the doctors in Chicago, are treating me as though that is what it is. Boy, that was a big mouthful to throw out at you quickly."

"I am so sorry for what you have been going through," she says, making me grateful I finally am talking to her. She adds, "I don't know if you were aware that MS was one of the possibilities the neurologist listed when you first had those tests."

"No. I didn't know." *So, Mom and Dad knew it might be MS. I wonder why neither she nor Dad mentioned this to me. Maybe it was because I never indicated I had any more symptoms. They might have thought I was fine, that the problem resolved itself.*

"Mom, I'm so sorry I didn't say anything all these years." I sit up very straight in my chair and fiddle with the ballpoint pen in my left hand. "I didn't want you to worry about me, and Dad would worry too . . . and you might worry about Dad . . . you know how antsy and emotional Dad got with illness in our family . . . and you had to live with him and deal with his worry, and . . . oh my, I'm so sorry that I'm dumping all of this on you right now." I move the phone from my right to left hand, realizing my fingers are stiff from clutching the phone so tight. *I say I'm sorry to dump, but I'm not, really. She's my mom and I have so much to tell her.*

"It's okay, Arlene. I understand your hesitancy. I know you were uncomfortable with your dad's worrying, his pacing. He cared about you so much and was just frustrated that he couldn't get a definite diagnosis."

My eyes fill up with water. *She gets it. I knew she would.*

"Thank you," I say softly. It is all I could muster to get out.

"I am just so sorry you kept all of this inside for so many years," Mom says. "But now that I know, I hope you will feel free to talk to me. I am here for you." My body feels limp, like a giant boulder has been lifted from my shoulders.

"That means so much to me, Mom. Only one more thing I want to say," I add, "why I am telling you right now."

My throat is so dry and my lips are starting to stick together that I get a glass of water as I start to talk, easy to do in my small kitchen, where the sink is only about four steps from my table and chair.

"I wanted so much to be at your birthday dinner at Monique's. I was not there because I was in Presbyterian/St. Luke's Hospital, hooked up to an intravenous drip. It had to be in-patient and during the night. I had so much time to think. I got so worked up that I didn't tell you the truth. It gave me headaches. I couldn't live with it anymore. I am just so sorry. So sorry."

I hear an audible sigh, a deep breath from the other end of the phone. Although only a few seconds, it seems like a vacuum, a long pause. Mom is relieved.

"Oh, Arlene, don't get down on yourself. I am so glad you called and got this off your chest. I'll support you in any way I can. Know that. Are you okay now?"

"Yes. I'm a little weak, but getting stronger," I answer. "That steroid treatment was to stop inflammation from intensifying. I think it's working. I'm able to drive and go to work."

"I am so glad you are getting better," she says. "No need to give me any more details now. You rest up and take care of yourself. Call when you need to."

Off the phone, I feel a huge sense of relief. A huge burden, one I created myself, is off my shoulders. I don't second-guess myself, ask myself if I should have said something years ago. Mom helped me feel okay about it. She knew what a big deal this call was for me.

◆　◆　◆

A few days later, on a Sunday morning, I'm sitting in the Fourth Church sanctuary during a worship service, singing with the large congregation and magnificent organ playing the hymn "O Jesus, I have promised . . ." I stop as a wave of calm sweeps through my body and my head wanders to a new place:

> Dad, I forgive you,
>
> for telling me how selfish I was in wanting to be an AFS student,
>
> for pressuring me to get married,
>
> for times you blamed Mom for things she had nothing to do with. . . .
>
> You did the best you could with what you were given. You were a good dad in so many ways, in providing and caring for us, even when you couldn't easily tell us that out loud. Dad, I forgive you and myself, too, for not understanding what you were going through. I know you cared deeply about me and loved me as your daughter.

I feel clarity and relief from the baggage I had been carrying about Dad. I feel love for him. That conversation with Mom, when I spilled out years of silence about my health issues, released me. It was as if I told Dad, too.

— CHAPTER 25 —

Promotion

Eight months after my cathartic phone call with Mom, I fly to Thailand over Thanksgiving to see Hilda, my former colleague from our work at the National Restaurant Association, where I worked right after grad school. Her husband is general manager of the Regent Bangkok Hotel, where I stay. Although in a big city, the vibe is slower. Spirit houses, looking like large bird houses on a tall stake, sit on many street corners. Locals stop, say a prayer, and then continue on their way. People stop to take off their shoes, enter a temple, and say their prayers at the base of a Buddha statue. Spirituality has no boundaries. It's visible on the streets here. Buddhist monks walk around in their beautiful burnt-orange and yellow robes. By osmosis, this spirituality seeps in and calms me.

I'm feeling great, not taking any medication, and have no qualms about taking a trip halfway around the world.

Now, back home in Chicago during the second week in December, I continue to feel energized from my trip. Visual images of splendid palaces, flowers everywhere, and fabulous food still fill my mind. In Thailand, I totally relaxed and didn't think about work. Being so refreshed, I throw myself into a myriad of issues facing me at work. My department is growing and I have increased responsibilities. I seize the opportunity to make my case for elevating my position to director.

This title change that I thought might be a slam dunk isn't. I receive pushback from my boss, who says the cap on the number of directors has topped out. He doesn't want to fight for it up the ladder. That seems like an artificial barrier. More likely, it's not been usual practice in human resources to promote women to this level.

I continue to advocate and push. This concerted effort reminds me of running for student council president in my senior year of high school. Three of my girlfriends asked if they could nominate me. No girl had ever run or maybe even thought about running. Knowing it would be a lot of work and maybe a tough fight, I wanted to think it through to make sure I wanted to throw my whole self into this effort. I said yes. It was a tough challenge that lasted a month, including speeches, making placards with slogans, recruiting surrogates to speak in public, and also talking one on one with the students. The pace was frenetic, and tension built. In the end, I won with many more votes than my opponent. We had a public celebration about this victory, not only for me but also for showing that girls can compete with boys for leadership positions. This experience reinforced the importance of advocating, not quitting, going up against opposing views to achieve a worthy and just goal.

My advocacy and perseverance regarding the director title pay off again all these years later. In March 1989, my new title, *Director of Human Resources*, becomes official. I believe that success is due to my presenting compelling data and already having shown my competence and value to the company. At forty years old, I'm now in the top 2 percent of management in a company of ninety-eight thousand employees.

— CHAPTER 26 —

Bold Moves

More than a year into my director position, the pace continues to be dizzying. Having purchased Pan American's international routes to Asia for $715 million in 1986, now in the fall of 1990 my company announces plans to buy Pan Am's London routes for $400 million, followed by a Boeing order of $22 billion in new aircraft. These numbers are staggering. Employees at all levels are talking about it. It's exciting, but what if there's an economic downturn? Is this amount of spending wise?

I feel the heat. In our hard-driving, doing-whatever-is-needed culture, we all keep going. If I would ever say I'm being asked to do too much, that would end my career. So I move forward. We have to find new talent for new positions, people who are capable of handling vast change and expansion. We need to educate ourselves on customs and regulations in countries that are new to our system.

In the middle of a gray November week, Peter and I plan to go to a new Cuban restaurant on the west side of Chicago. I arrive home from work at 7:30 p.m. with only forty-five minutes to change my clothes and meet Peter. I love midweek dinner outings because it breaks the pace, gets my mind off work.

As I'm standing in front of my bathroom mirror putting on lipstick, the phone rings.

"Hi, Arlene. This is Mark." *Oh no, my boss.* "I just got off the phone with our CEO. He wants a report on projected personnel costs versus budget for the rest of the quarter. And he wants it on his desk by nine tomorrow."

Think fast, Arlene.

"Mark, I'm just going out the door to dinner. This is a huge amount of work to complete by tomorrow morning."

"I know," he says with no emotion. "But we have to do it."

"Okay," I say, knowing my fun evening is canceled. I'm politically astute and know when I can push back and when I have to say "Okay."

I call Peter and tell him what just happened. He understands because he knows the pressure I'm under. He ends with what only a good friend could say: "The demands on you are relentless. You need a life."

I do need a life. I need more control over my time. With such a high-pressured job, how will I do that?

CHAPTER 27

Every Word Counts

The next day I get up at 5:00 a.m. and I'm out the door in forty-five minutes, having worked until 11:30 the night before, when my eyes started to blur over. I climb into my silver Saab and head to the office in a downpour.

Seated around our conference table, coffee in hand, my managers and I review the projections in our $12 million budget. It seems odd that our spending is being questioned when everything is going well and the company is growing. Is it that they're not making the projected profits? If we don't word everything correctly, I fear that some positions will be considered superfluous and people will be let go.

"The narrative we use is as important as the figures," I say. "We need to be clear and convincing about the *why* of what we're spending. Every word counts. I learned that in my first journalism class in college, and it's true." I'm well aware that part of what I'm saying is designed to help my staff learn what it takes to prepare a report for the top executive in the company.

I wonder what precipitated this request. This is not an idle exercise; I imagine decisions will be made based on these analyses that may affect employees' livelihoods.

What could save us at this moment is my ability to see many options in any given situation. My mind analyzes quickly, generating *we could do this* or *this and that*. I believe there's always a way to solve a problem, even if it takes a while. Very little is black and white. The assignment given to me seems on the surface to be straightforward, presenting estimated spending against budget. However, I know there must be underlying issues percolating, such as taking on more work without adding staff and analyzing if we have the right people in place to handle emerging issues involved with expansion.

I'm exhausted at the end of the day and ask myself if I could have done things differently. Peter's words ring in my ears, *You need a life*. Could I expend less energy, reduce stress? I've not had any neurological symptoms in two years, but getting run down could make me vulnerable. What can I do to reclaim a life outside of work and also reduce my stress at work?

– CHAPTER 28 –

The Best and the Brightest

"We want the best and the brightest," I say a week later, standing in the executive conference room, speaking to the top ten executives in the company. "We will work with you to assess whether key directors and managers are up to the new reality. With the results of the analysis, we will develop a plan of how to fairly coach each person, whether they will continue in their position or not."

The stakes are high for me in this presentation. The plan needs to be clear and the executives need to believe it will work. If I don't convince them of the worth of our plan, I will lose credibility and trust from those at the highest ranks of the company. My job will not be in jeopardy in the short term, but nothing is certain in this fast-changing environment.

The executives sit around an oval mahogany table, in black, leather-covered chairs that swivel. These men are used to meeting regularly with one another. A pitcher of ice water sits on a tin platter, with real glasses lined beside it. There are no pictures on the wall. It's formal and stark.

Obviously, I'm not one of the regulars.

Equal to the importance of developing and delivering an excellent presentation is how I look, my presence, how I articulate, the confidence I project. *Look directly at them, Arlene. Project that nervous energy into a strong voice that will command attention.*

"What should I wear?" I asked myself earlier this week as I gazed at the suit jackets and skirts in my closet. My mind flashed back twenty years to Minneapolis, carefully planning what I would wear on the first day of my first job out of college. I knew I needed to look professional, and that young women would be scrutinized more than the men.

Some things don't change. This appearance thing still seems to be more important for women than for men. Men comment on how women look in meetings, but I've never heard any man comment on another man's appearance. I'll be the only woman in the room. I'll not only look professional but also be on my A game, actually my A+ game, because there continues to be perceptions that women are not as strong, not as capable as men. A couple of days ago, two other director-level women and I were eating lunch in the employee cafeteria. One man we know came over to our table and said, "Something big must be in the works with the three of you talking together." Another man stopped by and said, "Three powerful women together. Are you plotting something?" We laughed, made small talk, then continued with our conversation about difficult management issues each of us is facing in this hectic time. We noted among ourselves that those comments would not have been made if three men had been sitting there.

"The best and the brightest," I say, making eye contact with each person. "That's what we in Human Resource Planning will help you attain."

Heads nod up and down. I have their attention.

"We stand ready to go, ready to work with you to make sure we have the right people in place to rise above the competition. We are a different airline, a global carrier, and we need to think and manage differently," I explain, wanting them to know I get it, get where we are and what needs to be done.

We conclude in the allotted forty-five minutes. I covered all the main points and didn't feel rushed. But do they get it? Do they really understand the upheaval ahead when managers are told they don't fit into the future of the airline? I can't chit-chat with these executives to get a pulse. I take a deep breath. Two senior VPs approach and thank me, telling me how clear the presentation was. I am pleased with how it went. I'm feeling strong as a leader and communicator in a pressure situation.

The rest of the day continues in a whirlwind. Around 3:00 p.m. I'm walking over to the Training Center for a meeting about a new customer service program when out of nowhere, a piercing pain, like an arrow, permeates the outside of my right leg. Since it has been two years with absolutely no symptoms, this pain deeply worries me.

I've done nothing to slow down. Maybe I've pushed my luck too far. I got through the best and the brightest speech with flying colors, but now my best and brightest self may have to face a health reality I've been able to ignore for a long time.

CHAPTER 29

Another Test

Ten days after the presentation to the executives, my life has taken a sharp turn to a hospital room. The jarring pain I encountered walking to the Training Center morphed into the familiar feeling, like hundreds of tiny needles piercing my legs. Feeling in my ankles swings back and forth from pain to numbness. Dr. D said prednisone won't help, so he orders a three-day steroid treatment, requiring an in-patient hospital stay. He also wants me to have a magnetic resonance imaging (MRI).

Drip. Drip. Drip. I stare at the bag that releases liquid, one drop at a time, slow and methodical. There's no other sound. It reminds me of looking out my bedroom window as a kid, watching an icicle hanging on from the eave of the house slowly melt, one drop at a time falling from the bottom point. It's mesmerizing and puts me in a daze. *Am I losing my health, one drip at a time? Maybe my condition is worse than I think and the doctors are hiding it from me. Get a grip, Arlene. This isn't a time to awfulize.*

My eyes drift up to check the big, round clock on the wall. It's 8:30 p.m. and I'm only a half hour into my eight-hour drip. Time marches on in silence. I turn on the TV. The picture has static lines running through it, but the sound is clear. Two men are talking about the war, projecting future outcomes and consequences. Although President George H. W. Bush declared a cease-fire after Kuwait was liberated in Desert Storm, the news channels continue to show pictures of tanks and fighter jets, rehashing what happened. I turn to another channel and find similar talk, so after a minute, the TV needs to click off. Silence will be healthier for my mind and body.

It's spring 1991, with plenty of turmoil in the world and within my own body.

I wake up the next morning thinking about work. Since my treatment ends at 8:00 a.m., I have all day to work by phone. Sitting in a big leather chair, I punch in Joyce's number on the beige touch-tone phone. Joyce is my go-to manager, who I ask to be in charge when I'm not in the office. We've worked closely together, and without exception, she keeps confidential information to herself. Plus, she's a clinical psychologist who knows how to be supportive while not being invasive.

She asks how I'm doing and says nobody is concerned because they think I'm on vacation. It's true. I am taking some vacation days to avoid any questions from my boss and staff. Joyce is the only person I've confided in about going through a treatment. My energy is strong and my head is clear. Talking with her, I'm in my comfort zone, asking questions, advising, and problem-solving. Joyce says my presentation to the executives is already paying off. Several meetings are scheduled with executives to start the process of assessing whether they have the right people in key positions.

Besides Joyce, my mother knows that I'm in the hospital. The minute I called to tell her about the need for a three-day steroid treatment, she said she would come to Chicago to be with me. For eight months she's been planning to fly to Tucson to see her grand-daughter Stacy. I pleaded with her to go because it would mean so much to both of them. Plus, she deserves some warmth and sun-shine after the long Midwest winter she's been through. Having said it was important for her to keep her plans, she decided to go and said she would call me each day.

◆ ◆ ◆

Midafternoon, I go for the MRI. This type of scan is relatively new and hasn't been available as an option for me until now. Dr D told me the MRI would take various pictures of my brain and provide more information from which the medical team can make a diagnosis.

"What's the test like? Is it difficult?" I ask my day nurse.

"You lie on your back in a tubelike machine. There's some clang-ing noises as the test progresses, and the technician will explain that to you. Some people feel claustrophobic, but don't worry about that. We'll help you relax and get through it," she assures me.

"I don't think I know anybody who's been through this test. Is it common?" I ask.

I'm concerned this might be something experimental, unproven, and I don't want to be a guinea pig.

"Its development and use increased in the late 1980s, but now it's becoming a common test in major hospitals across the United States. Many studies have been conducted and it's safe. We wouldn't have you go through it if it weren't."

An aide pushes me in a wheelchair down to the basement into a dim room that's cold. I lie still on my back as the MRI machine moves over me. I feel tense, as the technician tells me not to move an inch. My upper back starts to ache and my forehead itches. *Think of something pleasant, Arlene.* I picture a beautiful sunrise coming up over Lake Michigan. That distracts me, and after a half hour, it's over. I go back to my room for dinner, followed by a lonely evening with the steroid drip slowly entering my body.

Around 8:00 a.m. the next day, the nurse walks in the room, takes my blood pressure and temperature. She tells me that Dr. D will be here within a couple of hours with the results of my MRI.

About an hour and a half later, Dr. D enters the room with four residents following him. As usual, he's impeccably dressed, has no smile on his face, and is carrying a large envelope. The back of my neck tenses. They all look somber. Will the news be bad? I wonder if my brain has tumors or other abnormalities? This can't be good.

He remains standing, as do his residents, and announces matter-of-factly, "I have the results of your MRI. Let me show you the pictures." He reaches into the brown envelope and pulls out large, heavy, dark-colored sheets that look like X-rays to me. "See these little white spots on your brain?" he asks, pointing to them on the picture of my brain.

"Yes," I say, easily seeing them. This is the first time I've seen my brain. The image is dark, with a few white spots that mean nothing to me. Maybe these are small tumors that will grow? Heat rushes up my forehead. I'm scared. Will his next words about what these spots are devastate me? How I wish Mom was here to go through this with me. I urged her to go to Tucson and she's only a phone call away. I'll call her when these doctors leave.

"They are plaque," the doctor continues. "After careful analysis of these and all your pictures, plus all your symptoms over the years, this confirms what your medical team thought. Our diagnosis is multiple sclerosis."

I stare at him and don't say anything. In ten seconds, I hear two words that summarize all my debilitating symptoms and struggles for decades.

Oh, my God, it has taken twenty-one years to hear a definite diagnosis out loud. If they had known sooner, were there measures they could have taken to treat this better? And he's so matter-of-fact, without emotion. I wish my doctor would see me as a person and not solely as a test result. I feel like he punched me in the stomach, causing a deep ache. I feel like I'm a nonperson, an object that's being manipulated. I want to run out of the room.

As I look directly at the doctor, waiting for further information, he says, "I know it's taken a long time. The word 'multiple' is key with your condition, multiple symptoms that are hard to diagnose. You have one more drip, starting this evening, and will be released in the morning." Then he turns around and walks toward the door, his four residents trailing behind him.

I'm deflated. He didn't even ask if I have questions. I have lots of them. What's ahead for me? What's my future now that my doctor attached a definite MS label to my name? Is this drip-drip treatment all they have to offer me?

CHAPTER 30

Scaling the Mountain

After I leave the hospital in the spring of 1991, it takes three months to feel like myself again without pain. Meanwhile my company starts to lose money, caused by the Persian Gulf crisis and skyrocketing oil prices. Losses pile up, and by the end of 1992, United's loss is just short of $1 billion.

◆　◆　◆

Now in January 1993, in the span of a week, my right ankle weakens and I begin to limp. I call Dr. D, who prescribes a two-week regimen of prednisone. At work my boss says the Human Resources Division has to cut $325 million out of the budget.

My energy is low on a Monday morning as I get in my car to drive to work. For the first time in years, I grab my cane, just in case it's needed to keep me stable. With the cane in my right hand,

I walk out of my apartment, down the hall, and into the elevator. Having the cane makes me feel more stable. Yet I can't take this cane into work and reveal weakness, but it's helping me right now. The stress in the office will make me weaker since I'm already in a compromised position. Can I make it through the day? It's a must because I'm the key person to defend the budget for my department.

My head is foggy as I drive on to Interstate 90. I arrive at the office complex, park my car, and sit there feeling my leg and ankle ache. As I step out of my car, my right leg buckles. My body tips to the right as my knee bends. Whoa, I need to pay attention to my standing and walking so I don't fall. Walking through a sea of parked cars, I start to cross the road slowly, walking toward my office building. Only two or three people are leaving their cars and they aren't close. Good thing. Looking down, I focus all of my attention and energy on a two-inch curb. I need to scale this mountain to get to the sidewalk, then into my office building, but my right leg feels so heavy. *You can do it, Arlene. Lift that leg.* I take a deep breath and focus totally on lifting my right leg, but it doesn't budge. *Lift.* My heel comes up. I'm on the ball of my foot. I place my hand under my thigh and lift. Up comes my foot. I place it on the sidewalk. *Balance now.* I balance on my left foot and leg. *Once more, lift.* My right foot and leg finally make it up onto the sidewalk. Feeling fatigued from all the effort, I stand in place for a few seconds. My mind needs to be sharp today, at the top of my game. There's no way to be on top of my game, so I'll rally. I start walking—very slowly—toward the front entrance of the building.

The minute I get through the revolving door, tension fills the air. The executive offices reek of anxiety. Everyone knows and feels that layoffs are coming. Nobody is safe. Nobody. Sadness creeps into my psyche, sadness for all the promise of growth, of excitement for the future. Gone. Now it's the opposite: retrenchment, fear of job losses, every day filled with negativity.

I walk cautiously into the gray-walled conference room on the second floor near my office and immediately sit down at the oval table. The industrial relations director, a lanky, balding man, is pouring himself a cup of coffee. He looks tired. The lines near the corners of his mouth seem deeper, more pronounced than usual.

"Hi," he says, looking over at me. "I won't say 'Good morning,' because it won't be."

"Hi," I answer, lifting papers out of my briefcase. The vibe in the room is one of fearful anticipation. For weeks we've been working with Marketing, Finance, Airport Operation, and Maintenance on their plans for reducing costs. Now it's time for the Human Resources Division to do the same.

Zero Budgeting is today's buzzword—the reverse of cutting costs from a current budget. Start with zero as a budget on a blank sheet of paper and add in costs; that's our charge.

Mark appears in the doorway. He doesn't look directly at any of us. His gaze is blank. His starched, white shirt and red-striped tie look as formal and stiff as the task at hand. He moves quickly from the doorway into the room and takes his seat at the head of the table. All seven of us, almost in unison, turn our heads to look directly at him, waiting for his opening words.

"Okay, you've all done your homework," he says, diving right in. "Times are bad. We're bleeding money every day. Simply freezing salaries or taking a ten percent across-the-board won't get us to prosperity. That's why we are looking at eliminating programs and functions. Maybe entire departments."

The soft staccato whir coming through the ventilation duct cuts through the silence. I fidget in my chair. The only thing on my mind is hoping I can sit upright and seem to others like I'm normal.

My legs ache. Pins and needles jab into my pores. *Take a deep breath, Arlene. Focus.* My clear, analytical mind, which has served me so well in the past, is muddled by drugs this morning. Large doses of prednisone, meant to help my body rid itself of inflammation, are compromising my thinking. *I'll focus harder. I'll get through this.*

For the next two hours, one by one, we lay out our zero-budget plans. There's barely any discussion. It's not like finding a middle ground, you give some and I'll give some. We're all waiting to get lopped off at the knees. When it's my turn to present, all the preparation pays off. My written figures and rationale are succinct and clear, as are my oral comments. My body is giving out, but no one is noticing. I have to ignore my body, push mind over matter because what's most important right now is money, budget, my employees, my company. I feel the weight of my department on my shoulders, so that must be my priority, not my body.

I do a good enough job of pushing body issues to the side and focus my analytical mind and persuasive skills on the task to defend my department. I don't have time to think how long my body will hold out before it pushes back on me. I'll deal with that later.

The meeting concludes. The mood is solemn; it feels like someone died. We all know that cutting hundreds of millions of dollars out of our division's budget will have drastic consequences. Plus, the emotional energy we have all put into this complex process is immense and draining. I sit at the table shuffling through papers as others start to leave the room. My body feels weak, so I don't want to get up and start to wobble. Once everybody is out of the room, I stand up. My legs feel wobbly but strong enough to hold me up. I pick up my briefcase and walk out of the room.

The next step is for Mark and other division heads to make preliminary decisions on where to cut, then meet with the CEO. The bottom line is who will have their jobs and who will not. How will my employees be affected?

♦ ♦ ♦

One week passes. Mark's secretary tells us he wants to meet individually with each of us to go over decisions that have been made.

I enter Mark's office and sit down on a chair in front of his desk. He's frowning. How bad will his news be? I don't expect one positive thing to come out of his mouth. And I'm right.

"This has been very tough for all of us, Arlene," he says. "I won't beat around the bush. Your position, as well as all in Human Resource Planning, is being eliminated."

— CHAPTER 31 —

A Blurry Time

I gather my managers to deliver the bad news that we have six to eight weeks until our department disappears. Although not surprised, my staff stares at me in disbelief at the dramatic news. I think we were all expecting layoffs but not the elimination of an entire department. I mention what Mark said to me, "Drastic times call for drastic actions." That's little consolation and shows no empathy for employees affected.

The amazing thing to me is that, after the shock of hearing our department will be eliminated, my managers affirm their respect for me, my leadership, and my caring. They share with each other how much they liked working with our whole group.

We continue to talk, emote, explore the *what-ifs*. Despite our situation, we need to continue to work with other divisions on their layoffs, on repositioning people, on developing options, all in the midst of personal uncertainty. They have just had their jobs, their livelihoods, yanked out from under them.

Moving through the discussions with Mark and my staff is an out-of-body experience. I can't focus on my physical symptoms; my body is hurting, compromised. I focus for a moment on the aching in my legs and tell myself to ignore it until later. *Hang on, body. You can get through this.*

♦ ♦ ♦

One day blurs into the next. I'm putting in very long days and nights, and when not actually working, I'm thinking about it. All my waking hours are consumed by the implications and tasks related to the elimination of my department.

My mind is on a megadose of speed; a spike of adrenaline propels me forward. Contrast that with my body, a slow but determined tortoise, stopping intermittently to look around and assess what's going on. My mind races to figure out what will happen with my employees; my lethargic body wants to hide under the bed covers.

It's Saturday and I'm home, sitting at my desk. I look at my three-page list of employees, the white paper stark against the desk's teak wood. Who might retire? Who might transfer their skills into another division that might have openings? The information technology support my employees provide still needs to be done.

If only I felt better . . . if only I could clear my mind. . . .

I push myself up from the swivel chair and walk slowly into the living room to lie down on my couch. My body feels heavy, sinks into the softness of the wool cushions, and doesn't want to move. *Who on my list do I need to see? Who can I call? Perhaps I can do some of this work from here by phone. From my couch.*

The next day, Sunday, I don't do any work. I lie on my couch most of the day hoping my body will rebound a bit and my energy will last through this ordeal.

On Monday morning, I wake up at 6:00, sit up, then immediately lie back down. *A little more rest.* My mind has been racing throughout the night, problem-solving, wondering about the fate of my employees. An hour passes.

I leave my condo around 8:30 a.m. In my gray Honda, I'm on I-90 just past O'Hare airport when I feel a sudden thumping in my head, on both temples. I'm afraid I'm going to faint. Driving in the second lane from the left, I slow down to cross over four lanes to the right. *Focus, Arlene. Trust the rearview mirror.* My ears start ringing. I finally get all the way into the right lane, slow down, and aim for the shoulder ahead. I pull over, shove the gear into park, and put on my emergency blinkers.

I breathe in and out very quickly, lean my head back on the headrest, and close my eyes. This has never happened before. Am I going to lose consciousness? Will I be alone in the car for hours before someone realizes I'm here? *Slow down, Arlene. Take a deep breath . . . the day is just starting.*

Ten minutes pass. The pounding in my head and the ringing in my ears subside. I sit up and put the car back into Drive and hope this has been the worst thing that will happen today.

◆ ◆ ◆

I put in two months of twelve- to fourteen-hour days, working in the office and at home, first, the zero-based budgeting project, then working on placements for my staff. Finally, I cross the finish line. A few of my staff retire, but I manage to find at least temporary positions for all the rest.

Maybe I'll get repositioned elsewhere in the company. It doesn't matter. I've done what I needed to do. My focus has to be on my body now.

— CHAPTER 32 —

Limited Options

After weeks of pushing myself, I take some days off. I don't feel motivated to do much of anything. My body drags and my energy is depleted. The prednisone regimen is over and my leg strength rebounds.

Mark's secretary calls and tells me he wants to talk about my future next Monday. My future? *What* future? The department United recruited me to develop and lead is gone. I can't imagine anything that will interest me. I muster all the energy I can to get dressed. A lot of self-talk about breathing and putting mind over matter helps me get in my car and drive to the office.

"Good news," Mark says as I walk into his office. "I have a great job opportunity for you," he continues, then hesitates, waiting for some reaction from me. He doesn't get any. I can't imagine any news is good.

"I want you to be a staff executive for organizational effectiveness, in the Corporate Training department," he says. I sit there looking at him with no expression on my face. He has a big smile. I see pleasure in his eyes, like a kid being proud of himself for doing a good deed. Awkward silence fills the space.

Despite his big words, it's a demotion. I feel flattened, like a huge boulder just rolled over my body.

I don't jump at the "opportunity." I don't feign enthusiasm. Not at all. I'm skeptical.

"Thank you," I say politely. "What does this position entail? What are the responsibilities?"

He says this is a new position to "ensure the organization that is unfolding will meet the challenges the company faces to be better than the competition." To me, those are buzzwords. They sound good but are vague and hollow. What I think is that he's offering me a new position with a fancy title, but it's going to go from managing a big department to going solo with no authority and no staff. I want to say, "No way, this is a made-up job," but I hold my tongue. It won't help me to challenge Mark. His mind is made up and I'm politically savvy about what he's doing—he wants it to look like he's offered me a responsible position so he can tell the CEO that he found something acceptable for me. Then that task is crossed off the list.

"I wish you would say yes now, but if you need time, you can take it," he says. "Take a week to think about it and let me know." No surprises here, but the reality of hearing "staff executive" makes me angry. He just punched me in the stomach and landed a karate chop to my ego. Mark, who rarely shows empathy, is now playing nice guy, hoping I'll be grateful that he has a position just for me.

◆ ◆ ◆

At home, looking at myself in the mirror, I see small gray bags puff out under my eyes. My hair is out of sorts, hard to style in any reasonable way, since I've had no time to get a haircut in a couple of months. I look sad. No wonder, given what I've been through. I'm wiped out and just want to lie down on my couch.

◆ ◆ ◆

I don't want to accept that job. I want out. Maybe there's a way to get a severance package that includes health insurance. That's my primary concern and I've already checked with insurance companies about what it would cost to get my own coverage. The first question out of the mouths of the two people I contacted was "Do you have any preexisting conditions?" I said yes, and after mentioning the diagnosis of multiple sclerosis, there was silence. One agent said, "If you can get covered at all, which I doubt, it will be very expensive. It could be upwards of $10,000 a month. I don't know what your means are, but most people can't begin to afford it."

That's my reality and my label, uninsurable. Big insurance companies make the rules and are brick walls. I feel deflated, with no alternatives to look into. That's not me, though. I believe there are always options and I just haven't found them yet.

The week to think about it turns into two. When telling Mark I need more time, he doesn't push back at all. He gives me the time. I hire a lawyer with significant experience in developing severance packages, both for companies and for individuals. It's a long shot, because in my midforties I can't bridge to retirement. The only decent way to leave would be a buyout package, with a lump sum payment and continuing health insurance.

◆ ◆ ◆

What do I have to lose? Not much because my career has already been derailed. If I have to, I'll take the job, but my health is the number one priority. I'm looking into the future and the company is now a means to an end. There's no way to regain a healthy body in the midst of all the tension and chaos the company continues to go through. My lawyer contacts Mark with the proposal he prepared for me. In doing this, he needs to expose my MS diagnosis. Exposing my MS could be a good thing for me now. I'm hoping, given everything I've done for the company, that Mark will see what I've been dealing with and have enough empathy to agree to the package. When they're used to talking about millions, this kind of package won't be a blip on the company's radar screen. Mark's reaction is swift and predictable. He says there's no way to provide a buyout for me, particularly when he's offered me a new position. Now I imagine he sees me as a problem, someone trying to beat the system. What will he do? Will he try to retaliate?

The lawyer tells me that Mark is sticking with the position he proposed for me. That's the only option available. I formally accept the staff executive position—I'm trapped because I can't go without medical insurance. I tell myself to accept this reality, not ask *what if,* and don't let it sap more of the little energy I have.

CHAPTER 33

Dreary and Gray

This will be day three in the staff executive position. It's a dreary March day and I dread driving my gray car to a gray office, with gray walls, a gray-speckled linoleum floor, and a gray desk. I'm feeling tired even with seven hours of sleep.

◆ ◆ ◆

At 6:30 a.m., I climb into my car to start the trek to Elk Grove Village in the northwest suburbs. It's a typical morning commute on I-90. Stop. Go. Stop. Go. Stop. After an hour and a half, I arrive at the parking lot of the Training Center and walk into the same building where I started my first job at United nineteen years ago. Starting as a researcher, I developed innovative programs to evaluate employees' performance, received two promotions in two years, became the first and youngest manager in the New York office. After that, I created a new department from nothing, rose to director level, managed fifty-four employees, and received the Employee of the Year award. I thought when I hit the twenty-year mark, I'd be expanding my department further. The opposite reality faces me. It's all gone, everything ripped away from me.

After walking through the front door, I turn right and start down a long hallway. Nobody is around. Given that many jobs have been eliminated, there are a lot of empty offices. I slowly turn another corner, walk by three offices to mine. My brown leather briefcase doesn't feel heavy this morning. I'm so used to carrying it, a habit of my work life as a manager and director. This morning it's not filled with papers, not filled with work to be completed—a marker of my new status.

Sitting down on my black swivel chair, I wonder, *What will this day bring? What can I do that will be meaningful?*

I haven't seen a human yet. It's quiet, so different from the hustle and bustle I'm used to. There's been no direction given to me for this new position. They must figure that if I could create and build a new department from nothing, certainly I can figure out how to create a single position from nothing.

Lackluster describes my current state of mind. Maybe a cup of coffee will help. I stand up, go out the door, and walk to the tiny room with a coffee machine. I take my time in this tiny room, methodically pour some coffee from the pot into my ceramic mug, lean against the wall, and take a few sips. It's bitter and strong, as if the container holding the coffee grounds hasn't been cleaned in weeks.

Back in my office, there's a *While You Were Out* slip on my desk with a big WELCOME written on it from Jerry, who was my first supervisor at United. He is still here in the training department after forty-three years. What a downer. Jerry is fine, but this note throws me back to the first day I started at United.

I look at my watch. It's 9:20 a.m. and I've done nothing productive. I sit in my chair and stare at the dark computer screen on my desk in front of me. The power button is on top of a tower sitting on the floor beside my desk. I press it. A familiar little flashing light appears on the black screen as the computer boots up.

Letters and words appear on the screen. Is the computer out of focus? I lean over closer to the screen. The letters are blurry. Is there any way to make the letters bigger? I don't have a clue. I rub my eyes with the palms of my hands. I blink, then blink again. I look down at the memo pad on my desk, the one with my name on top and the familiar United tulip logo underneath. I got this special memo pad when I became a director. My name is bold, in big print. The letters are out of focus.

My life is out of focus.

I lean in, put my elbows on the desk, rest my head in my hands, and look straight ahead at nothing. I look up to see the clock on the wall. It's out of focus too. The second hand going around, and around, and around. I stare at it in a trance. My attention returns to the present. I can't just sit here. I need to do something. Attempting to stand up, my knees buckle; my right leg is weak. I catch myself by quickly grabbing the back of my chair.

What's happening? I'm totally losing it. Like kryptonite hitting Superman, rendering him totally useless, I'm compromised. But there is no meteorite hitting me from outside. It's all happening inside of me. Should I call for help? Since no one is around, it's going to take too much energy to find somebody. I'm alone, falling apart and scared that I'll collapse and hours later someone will find me out cold on the gray linoleum floor.

Focus, Arlene. Figure out what to do.

As I sit in my chair, my heavy eyelids close over my eyes. I don't feel faint. My heart isn't racing. It's not a panic attack, just unbelievable fatigue. My body is so heavy. I need to lie down, but I can't here in my office.

I slowly stand up again. *I have to get out of here.* Placing my hand on the wall steadies my balance. My legs hold me. That's a good thing.

I don't look for anybody. I have a blank brain. It's all a blur. Somehow, I walk to my car in the parking lot, drive twenty-six miles home, ride up the elevator to my condo on the eleventh floor. My body remembers what to do; I arrive home on autopilot.

As I open my front door, my mauve couch calls to me and my legs take me straight to that welcoming oasis. Collapsing on the couch, I stare at the ceiling. The wall clock says it's 12:40 p.m. My eyes slam shut.

CHAPTER 34

The Next Day

The next morning my eyes open. I roll over and look at the clock—7:40. I sit up and slowly dangle my legs over the edge of the bed. I feel like I've been hit by a truck. This is worse than bad jet lag, worse than a hangover, the worst fatigue ever. I feel like a Raggedy Ann doll, with little control over my arms and legs and little energy to sit up on my own for more than a few minutes.

I stand, and to my surprise, my legs hold me upright. I get dressed, make my bed, then walk into the living room and lie down on the couch. Every muscle in my body feels weak. If I rest, don't push myself, this should be over in a few days. *Stay positive* will be my mantra.

I call the office, say I'm not feeling well and can't come in. My credibility is good. Everybody knows I would not make something up to stay home from work. Why am I even thinking about what others' reactions will be? Why would someone question me? I need to stop ruminating about work when I feel so low.

After an hour, I muster enough energy to make myself a scrambled egg and some toast. Then I call Mom.

After I explain how I feel, she says, "Sorry you're feeling so fatigued. Have you had something to eat? Nourishment is important." That's Mom, making sure I'm eating well.

"I did, but now all I want to do is lie down."

"Do you want me to come to Chicago to help you out?" she says.

"Not right now. I want to see how I feel today and tomorrow." I want to put down the phone receiver; it feels so heavy in my hand. Mom has made me feel cared for. She's trying to be practical, make me feel better. But my body is so weary right now.

"Okay," she says. "Rest. The best thing you can do is rest. Are you going to call your doctor?"

"I'm not sure what he can do. I want to wait a couple of days." Mom is making sound suggestions and I resist because I don't want to make this a big deal. I want Mom to stay on the phone with me, but I want to be alone. My mind swirls with a bundle of conflicts.

I spend the day on my couch, not reading, not watching TV, just listening to WGN radio for entertainment. I don't feel sleepy, just have zero energy. My thoughts drift to my predicament. Why am I thinking about the office? Mark doesn't care. He didn't even react to learning I'm dealing with MS. I'm not needed and it doesn't make any difference if I'm there or not.

The next morning, I feel the same. My thoughts don't go far beyond wanting to lie on my couch.

◆　◆　◆

My friend Amy visits me after work. She comes in the door with a big smile, wearing a flowing teal-and-green caftan, and has a grocery bag in her arms. She brings me a large container of chicken noodle soup. That's Amy, so thoughtful.

Amy has flair. With a big, engaging personality, she is a leader whom everybody loves. We met three years ago over breakfast at the Drake Hotel in Chicago. As the CEO of Planned Parenthood in Chicago, she met me when I expressed interest in volunteering for her organization. Very interested in my background and expertise in human resources, she asked if I would consider being a candidate for her board. "Yes," I answered and joined the board two months later.

In addition to our many meetings together, we've become good friends. I can talk with Amy about anything and I feel comfortable admitting doubts and weaknesses with her. We often help each other think through and offer suggestions on solving difficult problems.

"Go ahead and lie down," she says. "I'll sit at the end of your couch by your feet. We have plenty of room."

As usual, Amy makes me feel better. Her voice is so soothing. We are both high achievers and we can laugh at ourselves about that. Around Amy, I don't take myself so seriously. I plump up my pillow to lie down facing Amy, who's at the other end.

"My mind is preoccupied with wanting to feel better, Amy. I want my mind to get clearer so it can figure out what to do."

"I know. I'm the same way, wanting to problem-solve to fix it," she says. "But maybe this will take a little time to figure out. Maybe you will have to sit with this for a few days." Amy's right, but it's hard for me to sit with it and not take some action. But what action to take?

She reminds me of the weekend seminar with Deepak Chopra we both attended a couple of years ago.

"Remember what he said, Arlene. 'We keep thinking the same thoughts. Today we rehash what we thought about yesterday, and tomorrow we'll rehash what we think about today,' he told us. That impacted me greatly, because sometimes we can't move forward, get out of a predicament. Somehow we have to clear those thoughts out and make room for new ones to come in."

"I still think about his words too. They hit where I am right now. I wonder how I can generate new thoughts about what to do in my situation."

Amy looks at me and laughs. "Hey, regardless of what happens in the next few days and weeks, make sure you have enough energy to get a pedicure. You love them so."

"Oh my, yes. Good for you to remind me to keep my priorities straight."

Although I don't feel better physically, I feel better mentally when Amy is around.

◆ ◆ ◆

The next morning, I call Mom and tell her about Amy's visit last night. "I'm so glad for your friend Amy. Plus, rest is good, Arlene. But you need to move around a little, get some fresh air. Why don't you at least go down to your lobby, then walk out the front door. Your doorman is there to help you."

"Good idea. I'm already getting tired of looking at my ceiling and walls. Thank goodness I can look out my windows at the expansive lake," I say.

"Also," Mom adds, "you need to call your neurologist. He needs to know where you are, and maybe he can help with the extreme fatigue you're experiencing."

Yay for Mom being Mom. I need that push. I need some direction right now.

Our call ends and I immediately make an appointment to see Dr. D early next week.

◆ ◆ ◆

I'm going to take Mom's advice and get some air. I put my keys into my jacket pocket. Unfamiliar anxiety swirls around in my head. I scratch my ear, the back of my neck. Going outside makes me nervous because I'll be on my own on the sidewalk. Can I maneuver without stumbling or falling? What if my knees buckle? *Get out the door, Arlene. You can do this.* I open my front door and facing me is the elevator. I push the down arrow.

I stare at those numbers as I go down: 11, 10, 9, 8. It's a familiar setting. I've gone down this elevator every day for thirteen years. This morning, though, it feels different. I feel a bit disoriented, so I place my hand on the wall to steady my body.

The door opens. There stands my kind, friendly doorman, facing me.

"Hi, Miss Faulk," he says, always respectful and formal. He is smiling and seems happy to see me. He must notice that I've lost my usual pep because he says, "Are you okay? You seem a little wobbly this morning."

"Nothing serious," I say. "But I'm experiencing horrible fatigue. I thought it might help to get some fresh air." I wonder if he doubts that it's nothing serious.

I go through the revolving door and step outside. The cool spring air hits my face. The bare trees and the stoplight at Lake Shore Drive and Division Street are a little out of focus. I cross the circular driveway in front of my building to the sidewalk and turn right. Although this is familiar territory, it feels foreign. Moving forward isn't easy. I fully concentrate on each step. Slowly, one foot in front of the other, I go a half block to the corner, Elm Street. *Should I cross the street?* I stand there contemplating. The answer becomes obvious. No. I can't go any farther. I need to lie down. I turn around and retrace my steps to my condo building.

I'm discouraged. My simple daily activities are arduous, labored. My usual mode of developing two or three options to move forward is stuck in the mud. How will my body return to normal in a few days?

— CHAPTER 35 —

Trying This . . .
Trying That

The following Tuesday, I'm facing Dr. D in his office.

"I've been hit by a tsunami of fatigue," I say, looking up at Dr. D, who is standing behind his desk, looking at me with no facial expression.

"This fatigue you're experiencing may be short-lived or may last a long time. There is no way to tell," he says, matter-of-factly. "I suggest you learn to live with it." His words knock my discouragement down a couple of notches. *Live with it.* He's supposed to help me find options. He's the doctor, for God's sake, and all he can say is *learn to live with it*. I don't want to learn to live with it.

I take a deep breath, gearing up to hear more of the same. "Many patients with MS suffer with the debilitating fatigue that you describe. Sometimes the fatigue lessens, but sometimes it gets worse. Fatigue can persist so intently that people can't walk at all and may have trouble sitting with a straight spine. Unfortunately, we don't have proven treatments that will absolutely lessen the fatigue. Before we deal with that, though, I noticed when you walked in, you were limping. Your right leg and ankle are weak. Let me examine you further."

After checking me, he says, "Here's a prescription for a ten-day prednisone and Pepcid regimen. I want to try to stop your exacerbation before going after the fatigue." I'm tired of the same old thing, a prescription for prednisone. The side effects are unpleasant and I'm concerned about long-term negative consequences. He brushes off my concern by saying that the medical team is very careful about prescribing the drug, using it only when needed to stop inflammation from ravaging my body. It's the most effective treatment available right now.

Before he finishes, he tells me he's going to get some research papers in two to three weeks on beta interferon, a new treatment for MS. He says I might be a candidate for it and it could be available as early as summer.

I feel weak when I get up from the chair. He just dashed my hope for some relief. He's so matter-of-fact, almost mechanical. I know his focus is research, but I wish just once he would show a personal touch.

◆ ◆ ◆

Here I am three weeks after leaving my office with overwhelming fatigue. My new boss knows about my MS. After concealing my physical challenges for years, I give her the okay to make my diagnosis public to coworkers. I call all six of my previous managers individually, because I know they will care. At least I don't have to think about income since my company has paid sick leave, which I asked to take because my return date to health is not known. The policy allows ninety days of sick leave, which should be more than enough time for me to regain my health.

But right now, having just seen Dr. D, I don't feel he's helping me move forward. There's no map, no compass I can use to move forward and return to work. This is a big test of patience.

I decide to work on the details of my new reality while reclining on my couch. I make notes on a yellow, lined pad, jotting down phone numbers of two neighborhood grocery stores that deliver. I phone a cleaning service and arrange for them to send someone out to clean my condo once a month.

That trip to my neurologist took all of the little energy I had left. *Now what?* Marshaling what little strength I have, I pull myself up from the soft cushions and make my way across the living room to my windows, my windows that allow me to see the expansive view of Lake Michigan, eleven floors below.

After an extremely busy day in the corporation, I used to find myself standing at these windows gazing out at the water. The various shades of blue—aqua, blue green, baby blue, navy—sometimes all visible at once, were mesmerizing. Still dressed in my navy, pin-striped suit and heels, I would feel the complexities of my day wash away. All my to-dos vanished from my mind.

Now, my days all look about the same. My routine is boring: get up, dress in jeans and a T-shirt, brush my teeth, then collapse on my couch. Around noon I have lunch. My meals are simple because I get so tired standing for more than ten to fifteen minutes. I might open a can of tuna, mix in some mayo, and make a sandwich. Then it's back to the couch. This was certainly not part of my career plan.

Maybe I can benefit from the experience of others. I'm feeling well enough most days to read for short periods. I ask Amy, Peter, Carol, David, and Mom for book recommendations. Maybe I'll get some inspiration. And if lucky, I might get a clue about what to do next.

I start with Bernie S. Siegel's book *Love, Medicine and Miracles*. He's fascinating, focusing on our ability to heal ourselves. Dr. Siegel talks about his own experience with a serious illness and how he turned to laughter to heal. I read Caroline Myss, Wayne Dyer, and Marianne Williamson. Common themes among these authors include love and determination. They help me realize it's a positive to be still, reflect, and not always be in an action mode. I learn that self-discoveries often come in silence. This is all helpful, but I hope it will lead me to a specific next step I can take to feel better.

In the midst of reading Deepak Chopra's *Perfect Health*, the phone rings. It's an Employee Relations specialist from work. She tells me that I need to apply to the Social Security Administration for supplemental security income, SSI. This is a mandatory step, she says, even if I later get long-term disability income from the company. If I qualify for SSI, that income will offset the income the company would have to pay. This is important from the company's standpoint to determine how much money they will have to pay me in addition to what the government pays. She's assuming I'm going to be out for a long time. I'm not. I'll be better soon and will return to work. But I call to get the forms, just in case.

◆ ◆ ◆

Two weeks later, on April 15, I'm back in Dr. D's office. It's a short appointment.

"It looks like your inflammation isn't getting worse. So now I'll deal with your fatigue and prescribe Symmetrel and Cylert," he says in his usual matter-of-fact manner. "About fifty percent of the people who take these drugs see improvement. You could be one of them."

Less than fifteen minutes after I entered his office, I leave.

One morning, the following week, I wake up and something feels different. My focus seems better and my head clearer. I stand up. Without hesitating, I search through my closet for my gray suit and white blouse, get dressed, eat leftover basil chicken, brush my teeth, and walk out the door. Driving the familiar route to my office, I reflect on why I'm doing this. It's certainly not because I'm excited about my new position. It's because I feel able-bodied and want to prove to myself that I can do this. I arrive at my office at 9:45 a.m. I don't see Mark or any of my former colleagues because they are all in other buildings. Three new colleagues are surprised but happy to see me. About 12:30 p.m., my legs weaken and I have to sit down. I'm foggy about what to do next. My mind swirls around with no focus. Fatigue completely overtakes my body.

My body is telling me this chapter of my life is closed. I can't go back; I will have to find a new direction. It's one thing to know it, but it's another thing to accept it.

— CHAPTER 36 —

The Lottery

Applying for Social Security benefits is a nightmare. I drag my body down to the Social Security Loop office. Although the May sun shines brightly outside, it's dark in this room. I can hardly keep my head up as I sit down. People are sprawled out on the uncomfortable vinyl chairs. It's stuffy.

My forms filled out, I wait for my number to be called. After an hour and a half, I go up to the window. The clerk behind it is busy with something and doesn't look up to acknowledge that I'm standing there.

I lean over, put my elbows on the ledge, rest my head in my hands. "Excuse me," I say. The slender clerk looks up at me and says in a monotone voice, "Sorry, I'm closing for lunch. Back at one thirty." And walks away.

So much for getting my application forms in today. I will mail them. I leave and take the bus home. Why do I have to go through this? It's degrading and impersonal.

A month later, in early June, Peter calls with an exciting offer. He calls frequently and gives me encouragement and this time he has an idea for me.

"You are not getting out much. Any way you might go with me to see the American Ballet Theatre at the Opera House in three weeks?"

"I don't know if I'll be able to, but I need to do something I love." The most motivating thing for me in the midst of this fatigue is to see ballet dancers or visualize track runners jumping high hurdles. They give me hope, not to be like them but to have a healthy, vibrant body. That's why I want to say yes, because it gives me hope.

My desire and excitement prevail and I don't care at the moment if my body will be strong enough to go. Peter will help me.

"Yes!" I say with the most enthusiasm I have felt in weeks. I long for something positive, for some hope. Over recent months I've had too many "I can't" moments. I need a moment of "I can." Maybe I can go to the ballet.

◆ ◆ ◆

"The Symmetrel and Cylert aren't lessening my fatigue," I tell Dr. D's assistant. I tell her that neither is making a difference. The side effects of bloating and a foggy mind make me feel worse. In addition to my fatigue, I feel drugged.

"Sorry to hear that, Arlene," she says, "but Dr. D wants you to finish the entire prescribed dosage." I'm really tired of hearing "sorry to hear that" from my medical professionals. Those words don't offer any authentic caring for me. Why can't they at least give me words of encouragement or some hope of moving forward?

The next week, my Employee Relations rep from work calls to tell me it's day ninety-one since I have officially been off work. I can now apply for long-term disability. She should have said *have* to apply, because it's a hurdle that seems daunting.

♦ ♦ ♦

On a sunny Wednesday morning in July, the phone rings. A nurse from Dr. D's office informs me that he would like me to come in this afternoon to talk about a possible new treatment. It's the beta interferon drug he was waiting for research data on, the drug that the University of Chicago researchers talked about last week.

I ride in a taxi to the hospital, walk into the bustling lobby, and head toward the elevators. I know my way well in this hospital. I ride up to the third floor and get myself down the short hallway to the MS Clinic. By the time I check in with the receptionist and make my way to a waiting room chair, a wave of fatigue sets in and I drop my head forward, closing my eyes.

"Arlene . . ." a man's voice cuts through the fog.

I look up to see Dr. D peering out from a doorway. I stand and follow him down the hallway.

As usual, his office is dimly lit. A few awkward seconds of silence pass. I cross my right leg over my left, change to left over right, then push the small of my back into the chair to sit up straighter. He starts speaking.

"There's a new treatment, self-injected by the patient, that's been going through clinical trials. It's a drug called Betaseron. I've reviewed all the research papers I received. The results of the trials have been so positive that the FDA is taking it through an expedited approval process. The initial doses will be distributed through a lottery, since the demand will be greater than the supply," he tells me. "I'll be getting a limited amount in about three weeks. You're a good candidate for this lottery. I need to know by Friday if you want this drug regimen, if you want to be in the initial lottery."

Friday is two days away.

"How long would I need to take Betaseron to know if it's making a difference?" I ask.

"That may vary by patient, so it is hard to give you a specific answer."

"What are the long-term effects, the downside after taking it for a while?"

"It's too early to have data on the long-term usage and effects. That study will have to occur in real time as patients are in the midst of the treatment."

This is a big decision for me. "You need to know by Friday. Wow, that's soon! If I don't do it now, I should be able to do it later, shouldn't I?" It shouldn't be now or never. I don't care to be a guinea pig of long-term consequences. I won't even be part of a study that keeps track of me. He's excited, but I'm cautious.

"Possibly," he says, although frankly, I think he looks surprised that I haven't already said yes.

"I can't make a decision right now," I tell him. "I have to think this through. I'll call you on Friday with my answer." For the doctor, it's a slam dunk. He finally has some positive news for me and I don't jump at it. I feel rushed, but not cornered. My decision will be my own.

My next two days are consumed with thinking the option over and talking with Mom, David, and Carol to get their opinions. They will support me whatever my decision is. What is the worst that can happen to me if I say no? More fatigue? More time on my couch? An unproductive life? What are the possibilities if I take the Betaseron? Who knows? Nobody.

◆ ◆ ◆

Two days later, on Friday, I talk with Dr. D and express my concern about unknown side effects and long-term impact of Betaseron. I calmly tell him no to participating in the lottery. I'm met with silence on his end. He asks if I'm sure, and I say yes.

◆ ◆ ◆

It's hard to believe, but a year passes as I continue to spend most of my days on the couch. In the fall of 1994, Amy calls me one evening. Her voice is soft and weak, very uncharacteristic of her. She says she woke up today and couldn't get out of bed. Fatigue overtook her body and her legs were stiff and wouldn't hold her up when she tried to stand. She knows I will understand because of the intense fatigue I've been experiencing for so long.

Over the next few weeks, Amy sees her internist, a neurologist, a cardiologist, and other specialists, enduring countless tests. No diagnosis from Western medicine, a puzzle without answers. Out of the blue, she received a suggestion that piqued her interest, an unexpected recommendation from a fellow CEO friend who had success in seeing a doctor of Chinese medicine.

Amy goes to see the doctor in the back room of a Chinese grocery store in Chinatown. He looks at her tongue and presses on her wrist pulses. His daughter is in the room, translating everything he's saying and doing and relaying Amy's comments to him.

The doctor gives Amy some raw herbs to boil for tea and recommends a person for *bodywork*, a vague term to Amy. He specifically wants her to see an acupuncturist and bodyworker named Nancy.

I listen intently to Amy's story, which is all new to me. Boiling twigs and leaves in a pot doesn't sound appealing. Amy is very enthusiastic, so I want to hear what she has to say.

I wonder where this is going.

"Nancy is helping me connect my busy mind with my body and I'm feeling great!" Amy says. "I can't tell you how much energy I have. The fatigue is gone. Arlene, why don't you make an appointment with Nancy?"

Amy waits for me to chime in. "I'll think about it, Amy," is my reply. I'm happy for Amy but don't understand how this would help me. My head is steeped in Western medicine, with my father and brother both physicians. I'm not tempted just yet to go that far into a medical approach so foreign to me.

◆ ◆ ◆

Another year marches on. No changes and no ideas on my next step. It's 1995 and I'm still asking, *Is this my new normal?* It has been for two years, but I hope for better soon. Stretched out on the couch, I look out the window. The deep blue sky is marked with a few wispy clouds. A sleek jumbo jet is turning west over the lake getting ready for an approach into O'Hare airport. I think back to when I worked for the airline, envisioning that I was on my way to bigger and better things. I imagined myself a world traveler—stopping long enough to experience daily life in another land. Strolling along the Champs-Élysées or enjoying pasta in the neighborhood trattoria in Rome, these are only in my head now, not in my reality.

My eyelids feel heavy and my eyes burn slightly. I close them—resting them along with my entire body—but I don't sleep. *Can it really be two years since that hot Friday when I phoned my neurologist to tell him I decided not to take part in the Betaseron lottery?*

Even with uncertainty in my body and future, I'm so glad to have waited. Data continues to be gathered, but initial reports show some negative patient reactions to the Betaseron. That may not have been my experience, but I still want another avenue to explore. I just don't know yet what it is.

Those last words Dr. D said to me are permanently imprinted in my mind. "Sorry, Arlene. There is nothing more I can do for you."

— CHAPTER 37 —

Mulling Things Over

During the last eighteen months, my most frequent destination has been my couch. I take daily notes, a diary of sorts. I don't feel much closer to figuring out what my future is. The unpredictability of my MS—not knowing how bad the fatigue, foggy mind, and any exacerbations will be—hampers my planning of any kind, including getting together with friends. I'm tentative and cautious, two words that had been foreign to me before the fatigue caused me to hit a wall.

I feel lonely some days, undesirable, unattractive, and, most of all, undependable. I can't promise anything, as I don't know if follow-through is possible. I'm frustrated with a life that has no purpose. Sadness fills my being. My existence is mundane.

My analytical and problem-solving skills, which always served me so well, aren't aiding me in figuring out what to do. Where are those new thoughts, new techniques for influencing my health in positive ways? Why can't I access them?

◆ ◆ ◆

Reclining on my couch, I relive that arduous SSI review process: filling out forms, dragging myself to the local office with no results, and later being made to see an impractical psychiatrist who asked me the difference between an apple and an orange. My application is denied based on the fact that I can dress myself, prepare a meal, and have normal cognitive function. Reading that feels like a slap in the face. Then my Employee Relations rep tells me the appeals process is relatively easy and recommends a couple of helpful resources to check out. I hire a lawyer whose practice solely focuses on Social Security disability benefits. Whether my appeal is approved or not, the monetary payment to me will be the same. I take the appeal anyway because it's a challenge and motivates me to call on skills I haven't used in a while.

"You're a slam dunk for getting a judge to reverse the initial denial," the lawyer tells me. "We'll work with you and we only get paid when you are approved." This seems like a no-brainer, getting professional guidance from a lawyer who does this work every day. I don't have a big emotional investment in this, but why not?

"Sounds good to me," I respond.

The lawyer prepares paperwork needed for the appeals review panel, represents me at every turn. The appeal is denied because the claimant, me, can sit upright for at least an hour at a time and converse on the phone. Therefore, the claimant needs to look for a job where talking without a need for any physical movement is possible.

The lawyer can't believe that decision. There's one final step, an appeal to an administrative law judge. My lawyer tells me it's extremely rare to get a decision overturned at that level. This lawyer who has told me she would be with me every step of the way dumps me.

I decide to go ahead and make the final appeal because I've nothing to lose. It's all in writing, no personal appearance. A written decision arrives in my mail. The appeal is denied. The reasoning given: *The claimant is able to make cold sales calls while lying on her couch. Therefore, she is employable.* Really? This is a ridiculous decision, so impersonal and unrealistic. I'm glad my livelihood isn't dependent on the decision of those judges.

◆ ◆ ◆

I do receive some good news. My company approves long-term disability (LTD), retroactive to day ninety-one when I officially stopped work. I'm happy about this decision. It takes pressure off me to earn an income, and the company disability benefits package is generous. Once LTD is approved, it lasts until I'm sixty-five years old.
It's a relief not to worry about money, but that alone is not enough. I'm only forty-seven years old and I want to be productive. What am I going to do? How can I find purpose in the rest of my life?

Mom calls every week to check on me, hear how I'm doing. She always cheers me on with her wise advice like "Don't focus on what you can't do. Focus on what you can do." She is so happy the appeals process is over because that only drags my energy down. Carol, David, and Peter call to see how I'm feeling, physically and psychologically. Dena keeps tabs on me too. And of course, Amy. I talk to her a couple of times a week. Talking with Amy always includes laughter, which I love. It lightens things up.

Just this week, a card arrives in the mail from Amy. Inside the card, a handwritten note simply says, *A Gentle Reminder.* There's a business card attached. Lying on my couch with my friend's note on my lap, I acknowledge that I've been off work for two years and

I think the same thoughts, not new ones. I've taken no risks. *I've always been a doer. A problem-solver. Why have I done so little about my health these past two years since turning down the Betaseron trial? Why haven't I done something, anything to move forward?* I realize I have to take a step forward.

Immediately, I get up from the couch, go to the kitchen, and dial the number on the business card, Nancy's number.

Nancy's voicemail kicks in. I hear her calm, soothing voice. With more vigor than I've had in a while, I spill out, "Hi, Nancy. I'm not sure what you do, but my good friend Amy speaks highly of you. I'd like to have more energy, and if I can't have more, I'd like to use the energy I have more effectively. I'd like to make an appointment to see you."

CHAPTER 38

Meeting Nancy

No way. No way I can do this. My jaw clenches. I sit motionless in my car, staring at the eight steep steps of concrete I have to climb to reach the front door of the brownstone building that is my destination. How is it that I was able to tediously get myself dressed and drive over here, but now have to contend with this? I pull out the yellow three-by-five index card I wrote the address on, just to make sure. Yes, this is the right address.

What am I in for? Am I doing the right thing? When Nancy returned my call, her voice was caring and inviting, and I was encouraged to go ahead and make an appointment. But at this moment I'm anxious and feel unsure about my decision.

♦ ♦ ♦

I'm facing a familiar roadblock—steps. I'm ready to meet Nancy and am so close to getting there. In fact, I'm here. I just have to figure out how to get up those steps and inside the door.

After exiting my car, I look down to make sure I don't step on a tree branch or a rock that would throw me off-balance. I walk furtively toward the steps. A two-inch-wide, black iron railing on the left side of the steps eases my anxiety. Clutching my cane in my right hand and putting all my weight on my right leg, I pick up my left leg. *One step at a time, Arlene, just one step.* My hand grips the railing. I stop, put my weight on my left leg, reach down, put my right hand under my right thigh, and guide my leg up to the step. It's a little awkward because my cane is still in my right hand.

One by one, I meticulously move up these steps, placing my weight on my left leg. Now on the top one, I take a deep breath. I made it! As I stand there silently celebrating my victory, the door slowly opens.

A woman's face appears in the doorway.

"Hi, Arlene. I'm Nancy. I'm so sorry about these steps. Come in."

As I take a step inside the front door, Nancy, with a big smile and reassuring voice, says, "Come this way. You don't have to walk far."

We walk into a warm room, with a massage table and two chairs, which face each other. Nancy has chestnut-brown hair, falling just below her ears. She wears yellow-and-gray patterned shorts with a matching flowy top.

"Please have a seat, Arlene," Nancy says as she picks up a clipboard with paperwork on it and grabs a pen.

"I'm so glad you made it here," she says, looking directly into my eyes. I notice how blue her eyes are.

"I am too, Nancy." I'm very engaged and curious about what will happen next.

◆ ◆ ◆

It's quiet, calm. I smell the hint of a pleasant scent in the room. It's definitely not incense. It is lighter, familiar, yet I can't name it.

"Nancy, what's that nice aroma? I like it."

"It's lavender, a touch of lavender oil that I use. It's very calming and soothing."

I'm in a straight-backed chair, facing Nancy. Looking right into my eyes, she says, "I know you said in your voicemail that you want more energy. Let's talk about the past a bit and build up to the present. Is that okay with you?" She continues to keep eye contact with me.

"Sure," I respond. My gaze veers away for a few seconds. I glimpse framed Chinese calligraphy on the wall—bold, black ink strokes with what looks like an upstroke of the brush on the right side. It is on white paper. Maybe it is rice paper? I wonder what it says.

I catch myself and return to look at Nancy as she continues, "First, I'll give you a brief overview. This appointment will be an intake, gathering information about you, about your background, including family, medical history, briefly about your jobs and career. Then I would like to hear how you feel about where you are and any goals you might have right now. I'm not a psychologist, so this is not therapy. It's helpful for me to deal with the whole person. That's what Chinese medicine does, deals with the whole person and root causes rather than symptoms. Ready to start?"

"Yes."

"Just talk about what you are comfortable with. At the end of our conversation, you can decide if you want to make an appointment for a treatment."

Already Nancy has spent more time with me than my neurologist did during our last two appointments combined. Plus, she did not start by asking about my current symptoms, as my neurologist always does.

"I would like to know a little about your family," Nancy says. "Did you grow up with a mother and father at home? Any siblings?"

I answer factually, wondering where she is going with this.

"Were you healthy as a child? Any prolonged illnesses? Traumas?"

Answers to those questions are short. Yes. No. No.

"What are you experiencing right now?" Nancy asks, jumping back into the present.

What I'm experiencing right now is being totally captivated by Nancy. I feel warmth and compassion that I've never experienced before in the presence of the myriad of doctors I've seen over many years. Her voice is strong and reassuring, like my mother's was when I spilled out my MS secrets to her over the phone a few years ago. Without saying the words, I heard Mom say "I am with you." This is what I hear from Nancy right now.

"Fatigue," I say. "After being in a fast-paced job and career, always on the go, I've spent the last two years lying on my couch. What a drag," I say, surprising myself by admitting that it's been two years.

"I also feel weakness in my right leg and ankle. Right now, my legs and ankles are strong enough to hold my body weight and also walk with the aid of my cane. Nancy, I need to stand up for a moment. My right foot feels like it's falling asleep. I never know when I feel this sensation if it is falling asleep or actually going numb. Sometimes it starts with intense tingling, then aching, then no feeling at all."

"Okay, Arlene. Get up and walk around a little. Would it help to hold my arm to steady you?"

"Thanks, but no." I'm fine in this small room and I have my cane. I lift my right foot off the floor and turn my ankle in circles before standing. Once up, I take a couple of steps, then stop. Then I take a few more toward the door.

"Ah, the feeling is coming back. I'm so glad," I say with a sigh of relief.

"Now tell me when and how this all started," Nancy says, propelling me back twenty-five years to 1970, that afternoon when I lost all the feeling from my waist down.

On and on, the questions and answers go back and forth. Nancy asks and I do my best to answer. Frankly, I'm amazed. How does Nancy sit there writing copious notes and also keep such good eye contact? She is so present, actively listening to me. She seems to be with me, in my space, in my experience. She's not missing a beat.

Two hours pass. Nancy says she is ready to wrap up.

"Any questions?" she asks.

"What's next?" is the only question that comes to my mind.

"I'm moving to a temporary office in downtown Evanston. If you would like to move forward and schedule an appointment for a treatment, we'll meet there next month."

"What does a treatment include?" I ask, uncertain about what this means.

"You'll get on a massage table and I'll work with my hands on your body to stimulate energy points. I have something to give you that might help explain."

She gets up, walks to a table, and picks up a stapled handful of papers. I watch her, but I'm in my own thoughts. I've had massages before, some deep tissue, others more superficial. Nancy said massage table, but not that the treatment will be a massage. I have a hunch about her. She will not do anything to set me back and maybe she will help. Maybe Nancy really can help me.

She brings the papers to me, an eight-page article on the Five Element theory, and tells me this might help me understand some basic concepts of Chinese medicine, on which the treatment will be based.

"Would you like to make an appointment in September?"

As good of a vibe as I get from Nancy, I still feel guarded and don't know what she can possibly do to help me. But I'll be back in nowhere land if I say no.

"Yes," I say, knowing I can cancel if I change my mind. Nancy smiles and reminds me what a big step I have taken today, to drive to her office, get up those steep steps to the brownstone, and meet with her. She applauds my courage.

CHAPTER 39

It's a Process

"Working with your body to help it heal itself takes time," Nancy explains before the hands-on treatment. "It's not like taking an aspirin to lessen a headache. It's a process rather than targeting a specific symptom or area of the body." She looks at my tongue, top side and underneath. She takes both my wrists and says she wants to listen to my pulses. I listen to her, although it is not clicking yet. I do not understand what she will be doing on the massage table. But I do understand *process*.

I don't remember anyone talking directly to my body before. The closest was many years ago when Melody said, "Your body doesn't lie."

♦ ♦ ♦

Alone and naked, I sit on the edge of the massage table, scoot back a bit, and slowly bring my legs up, then roll onto my side to bring my entire body on the table. I lift the white sheet and roll under it, facedown. Pulling myself up toward the end of the table, I place my face in the small, cloth-covered cradle. With my face pointing downward, my nose begins to stuff up immediately.

A soft knock comes from the other side of the door.

"Are you ready?" Nancy says as she slowly cracks the door open.

"I'm ready." Although, frankly, I'm not sure what it is I am ready for.

"Are you comfortable?" she asks, entering the room. *My nose is stuffed up. I don't know what to do with my arms. My legs ache. My shoulders are up to my neck.*

"Yes," I answer.

♦ ♦ ♦

Nancy lifts up the top part of the sheet that covers me. She folds it down to my hips, to expose my back. I feel a little chill when the air hits my bare back.

"Take a big breath in," Nancy instructs me, "inhaling white, shimmering Da Qi—energy of the air—expanding your lungs. And now exhale any dark, thick, stagnant energy out of your body."

I exhale and feel her fingers pressing firmly on two points on either side of my spine. "Breathe in. Breathe out," she says while very slowly and methodically pressing additional points on my back, a pair at a time, from my neck to my tailbone.

"This is the gallbladder channel," she says, moving on to press her hands against the outside of my legs. "The Qi, your life-force energy, is blocked. I can feel the blockage with my hands. I am trying to open up points so the Qi can flow better along the channels," she explains. As she continues working on my legs, I try to keep my mind open, try not to analyze. I'm puzzled, though, because I don't understand what she is talking about. *Qi? Pressing points? Gallbladder channel? Oh, the pain in my legs has lessened, just for a few seconds.*

I try to pay attention to Nancy's pressing points on my feet, but my mind drifts to her words during our long intake interview.

"Your body is hurting, Arlene. It's been going through so much for a very long time." Her words continue to resonate. "You didn't tell anybody for so long. You kept it a secret. Secrets, keeping the pain and emotional stress locked up inside, can take a toll on your body."

Hearing this is a first for me, a recognition that keeping secrets has consequences. Maybe keeping secrets is part of why I ended up lying for two years on my couch. My reasons were valid—I thought my career would be jeopardized if I said anything. I would be seen as weak, unable to keep up with the intense pressure.

I never told Dad about my struggles; I thought if I told him my secrets, he would worry, be anxious. Yet I copied his pattern. Like Dad, I thought keeping secrets would prevent other people's sadness and worry, but in fact that's not the case. Keeping secrets from others has harmed my body.

I wonder if Dad's secret past caused him heart problems. He buried so much inside that was painful, and I've buried my MS for over twenty-one years.

Through my brief connection with Nancy, I realize the cost of keeping a secret for years. I made excuses about why I wasn't at work as I was tied to a steroid drip in the hospital. I went to my doctor's appointments, to my CT scans by myself. I thought I was making good decisions, coping, and being a successful businesswoman by not appearing weak. My mind kept pushing me, and my body finally told me I've been doing great harm to my health.

◆ ◆ ◆

"Okay, Arlene. We're finished with the treatment. Go ahead and put your clothes back on. I'll step outside and come back in a few moments."

When she returns, she comes to me as I sit fully clothed on the edge of the massage table. She gives me a hug and hands me a paper cup of water.

"I suggest you sit in the waiting room for a few minutes before venturing out. Take your time," Nancy says with her reassuring voice, looking directly into my eyes.

Sitting in the waiting room, I feel calm and happy I've met Nancy. I'm not sure what the treatment is doing for my body, but Nancy did give me things to think about. Finally, I'm starting to get some new thoughts into my head. I'm not sure what's next, but Nancy says it's a process. I'm okay with that.

Today is step one.

CHAPTER 40

Needles

Yes, it's a process. Nancy suggests I need to be kind to my body and be patient. That often replays in my mind—when I wake up in the morning, when I eat lunch, when I sit on my couch, when I venture out for a short walk in my neighborhood. Getting outside feels like progress, but there's worry in my mind about when the fatigue and pain will come back.

Time. I think about time, talk about it with Peter, with Amy. How is it that we all have twenty-four hours in our day, but our experience of time speeds up, slows down, or stops depending on our emotional state? Not getting a specific diagnosis for twenty-one years seems unbelievably long, but in those years, I was busy with my career, friends, and travel. So the time it took to get a diagnosis only seems long in retrospect. I wasn't sitting around waiting for it.

On the other hand, two years spent lying on the couch seems extremely slow. Living with the uncertainty of whether my body will work right—whether I can walk out the door and down the street and if I will at some point be free from pain—makes time drag for me.

I deal with that time drag, in part, by taking up needlepoint. I always admired Mom's skill at it. She meticulously and expertly did needlepoint on seat cushions for six straight-backed chairs, a maroon background with pretty light-colored flowers in the middle. I admire them even more when I start my own needlepoint pictures. It takes about an hour to complete one inch. Talk about slow! But I find it very satisfying because I'm using my hands and I'm accomplishing something.

Needlepoint takes time. Nancy reminds me healing takes time. She says it out loud, sets realistic expectations for me. Plus, she's willing to walk with me through this uncertainty, willing to work with me to get better. I like that. It brings me comfort. Nancy also tells me this is a partnership; we're working together. I'm not sure what she means because I'm still on a table as she works on me with her hands. How am I a partner?

Nancy suggests a goal. "Let's see if we can turn your current one-step-forward-two-backward to two-steps-forward-one-backward." I embrace that goal and commit to working with Nancy an hour and a half every other week. *Great, a goal. Something specific to work toward. Nancy gets me. She knows that goals motivate me and put me in a comfort zone.*

♦ ♦ ♦

A month later, during my third appointment, Nancy starts with her hands pressed into points on my back, asking me, as always, to breathe in shimmering Da Qi and exhale any dark, stagnant energy out of my body. After a few minutes, she asks me to turn over on my back.

"Are you okay with me using acupuncture needles?" she asks.

"Yes," I answer. "This is my first time. Just tell me what you're doing. Knowing will help me relax."

"The needles stimulate the same points I've been working on with my hands," Nancy explains as she inserts four needles into each of my legs. "The needles are very thin, almost as thin as a strand of hair." *Will they hurt? How long do they stay in? How will they help me?*

Surprisingly, they don't hurt. I don't feel anything. "I'll continue to press specific points with my hands, even as the needles are in," she adds. "Are you doing okay?"

"Yes," I answer.

"Okay, I'm going to leave the room for a few minutes to let the needles do their work. I'll put some music on to help you relax." It's dark in the room and I close my eyes. My forehead starts to itch. I think Nancy placed a needle in the middle of my forehead, so I don't want to bother it. *Breathe, Arlene, breathe.* My right shoulder aches. I'm not releasing. *I hope Nancy comes back into the room soon.*

Twenty or twenty-five minutes later, the treatment is over. Nancy removes the needles. I dress. She gives me a glass of water and asks me to sit for a few minutes in the waiting room before I leave. I sit there, look at the big corkboard across from me, filled with all kinds of flyers held in place with pushpins. It's quiet. I feel a little dazed.

Suddenly, I feel a little chill in the back of my neck. I realize the pain in my legs is gone. The aching has decreased. How could those needles work so fast? Am I imagining this?

♦ ♦ ♦

Four hours later, I'm on my couch engrossed in a John Grisham thriller when my legs begin aching. The pain intensifies quickly to sharp needlelike pain. My legs feel like they are plugged into an electric socket.

"This is awful!" I exclaim out loud as I pace around the room. I call Nancy's office and get her answering machine. I circle around the living room. I'm scared this could get worse. *Please call, Nancy. Please call soon.*

Within a half hour, Nancy returns my call. "I'm so sorry that you're in such pain," she says. "It sounds as if the acupuncture was too strong, too invasive. Try using your fingers to put pressure up and down the outside of your legs."

"I'll try anything at this point," I say, feeling desperate. I scrunch the phone up by my left ear, freeing both hands, then follow Nancy's instructions and press as hard as I can.

"Call me in the morning to let me know how you feel," Nancy says. *I wish she wouldn't leave me. She knows what to do and I don't.* But even with the pain, I feel she really cares. For such a long time, I had simply felt like a body on a table.

For the next hour, I sit in the middle of the floor, methodically pressing the outside of both legs, from my knees to my ankles. *This feels like a big setback.* Gradually, over another hour, the pain subsides to a dull ache. It's finally tolerable. But I'm weak and exhausted.

I climb into bed, hoping for sleep through the night. *Am I doing the right thing? I hoped Nancy could help me. Can she? Is there anybody out there who can give me hope? I feel so alone.*

CHAPTER 41

Something New to Try That's Old

Why do I go back to see Nancy? I definitely question whether I should. But I want some answers, some reasons why I had such a severe reaction to my treatment. There's no way I can figure that out on my own. I need Nancy's perspective. Plus, I still have a hunch. I hear Amy's voice whispering in my ear, *Maybe Nancy can help you.*

Three days after that scary evening, Nancy fits me into her schedule. She's concerned about me, troubled by the violent reaction my body experienced. I return because she wants to hear more about the experience, figure out what might have happened, and determine an appropriate approach to move forward.

I'm glad she fit me in because she's going to be away for three months. After four years of traditional Chinese medicine study at the Midwest College for Oriental Medicine, she's leaving in November for intensive study in China, which includes work in clinics and hospitals to hone her knowledge and technical skills.

"Feeling like you were plugged into an electric socket gives me a graphic picture of what it must have felt like," Nancy says, facing me in her office. "I'm so sorry, for you and for your body."

"Me too, Nancy. It was awful."

"It's obvious that acupuncture is too strong for you right now. I won't use needles. I'll work with my hands, very gently. Is that okay?" She doesn't spend time analyzing. She must know my body is not ready for the energy unleashed by the needles. She has thought this through. She has a plan B.

"Yes, gentle sounds good," I reply.

While I'm on the table, Nancy is so kind to me and careful in her work. It feels like I'm receiving a gentle, reassuring massage. She presses on the outside of my knees, my back, my feet, and even some points on my head. She tells me of the tension she feels in my body and says I have stagnant Qi. "You need to rest. You need to drink lots more water. You shouldn't push yourself to do anything strenuous." *I'm glad to be here. She really cares about me.*

Unlike the usual me, I don't spend much time analyzing the scary evening. This session with Nancy puts me in a different place, determined to keep trying. I make an appointment to see Nancy the week after she returns.

♦ ♦ ♦

After a stable three months on my own, I return to see Nancy, excited to hear about her education and experiences in China.

"Arlene, I'm ready," I hear as the office door opens. I feel more relaxed just hearing Nancy's voice. I stand, and as I walk toward the door, I'm greeted by Nancy's smiling face. She gives me a big, firm hug. It's March 1996. Even with a chill still lingering in the spring air of Evanston, I feel warmth as her welcoming Qi envelopes me.

"Nancy, I'm excited to hear about your work in China. You look great!"

"It was amazing!" She is energized, but calm and centered, as though all is right in her world.

Nancy tells me she worked with Chinese doctors and teachers to learn about procedures and interventions based on both Chinese and Western medicine. Chinese doctors and patients do not use the term *multiple sclerosis*. That is a label in our Western culture. She had opportunities to talk with patients through an interpreter. Patients carry a manila folder around with them—their medical records. All in one place. She visited with women and men in their seventies and eighties who had what we call MS, and they were walking around with a normal gait. Two men proudly opened their manila folder and showed Nancy pictures depicting them using a cane. One woman showed her a picture of the time she was in a wheelchair. Did Nancy discover something that will help me? I lean over closer to her, hanging on every word.

Nancy says she was curious. "I asked them one by one, what do you attribute your current good health to, after years of not being able to walk without assistance?

"I was amazed at the consistency of their responses, with three definite themes: one, diet; two, bodywork; and three, Tai Chi."

Nancy pauses for a few seconds, looks directly at me with her eyes wide open, eyebrows arched up. "There's no magic pill, no one thing that may work for everybody. We know that. However, you already have a healthy diet and have embarked on a path with bodywork, so why not look into Tai Chi?"

All I know about Tai Chi is that it is a martial art originating in China many centuries ago. That's it. Not a great start. Where do I find a good Tai Chi instructor in Chicago? How do I evaluate if the class is good and right for me? Will a teacher understand if I can't do everything other students can do?

– CHAPTER 42 –

The Energy Ball

Later, it hits me—I do have a lead. My church has a very robust program for older adults that includes Tai Chi. I call the program director, an approachable, kind woman, and ask her if I can observe the class. Not only does she tell me I can observe the seniors' Tai Chi class, but she also says I can participate if I want to. She knows about my physical struggles and doesn't say I'm too young to join. I'm forty-seven years old and I'll be the youngest in the class by decades, but I'm willing to try just about anything.

On a Tuesday afternoon in the spring of 1996, I slowly walk out the front door of my building to the bus stop by the curb. The 151 bus arrives in five minutes. At the fifth stop, only a few blocks away, I exit the bus, using my cane to stabilize me.

Suddenly, I have doubts. My body might be too weak to keep up. *What if I am not ready for this? How much will I be able to do?* Then, just as suddenly, my can-do Arlene mind turns on, says go, and propels me forward into the church building.

◆ ◆ ◆

I make my way to the large room used as the church social hall and spot small groups of two or three women each chatting. I don't think anybody notices me as I walk in with my sturdy cane in my right hand. A fit Chinese woman with short, black hair enters from the hallway and comes directly toward me. Her posture is great and she is energetic.

"Hi. I'm the teacher," she says, stretching out her arm to shake my hand. "Arlene? Welcome. The director told me you might be coming."

She grabs a gray metal folding chair and tells me it's fine to sit for class as much as I need to. I do need that chair and am glad to have permission to sit. As the teacher moves to the front of the room, the fifteen women and one man find their places in the middle of the room. Class is ready to start.

I quickly size up the group—short, tall, limber, stiff. The tiny woman with reddish hair has two metal canes that she puts on the floor beside where she stands. Her name is Reggi. As she starts Tai Chi, her moves are fluid and her balance seems good. Amazing. She and all these people are considerably older than I am, by as much as thirty to forty years.

Will I embarrass myself if I can't do the moves? Stay open, Arlene. Just go with it.

◆ ◆ ◆

The folding chair I'm sitting on is in the left back corner. I can see the teacher around the others, who are standing.

"Stand with your legs and feet about hip-width apart," the teacher instructs. Most students look down at their feet as they get

170

in *ready* position. "Knees are soft. We don't want to lock our knees. Now place the palms of your hands on your lower abdomen, thumbs touching at your belly button, index fingers pointing downward to make an inverted triangle.

"We're learning to breathe from here, from the tan t'ien, our center of gravity, where our index fingers meet about two and a half inches below the belly button," the teacher explains. "Imagine a tiny baby breathing, her little tummy naturally expanding, in and out, in and out. This is the essence of Tai Chi," she says as we continue to breathe. "When we practice Tai Chi, we are returning to the energy source we are born with."

I'm not sure what she means, but I sit and continue to breathe. *Hmm . . . essence, return to the source.* This is new to me. I take it in but have nothing to compare this to. I wonder how this might help me. *Oh, Arlene, bring your attention back to your breathing.*

"Now, inhale while raising your arms straight out in front of you, up to chest level. Lower your elbows, bringing your forearms toward you, palms of your hands facing each other, like you are holding a ball. Imagine the ball is the size of a beach ball, lightweight, filled with molecules constantly in motion," the teacher says.

All arms in the room, including my own, grasp an invisible ball at chest level. "Inhale and expand your energy ball. Exhale and contract the ball." Seated in my chair, I scoot myself to the front edge of the seat, not sure where to look. I decide to focus on the empty space between my hands.

In and out my breath goes, with my hands barely moving. Time disappears. I'm concentrating only on this ball.

"Working with this energy ball can be helpful for balance, for increasing awareness of your own energy," I hear the teacher say, momentarily interrupting my trance. My back feels tired, but I keep going. *Sit up straight, Arlene. Concentrate on breathing.*

Next the teacher has the group focus on walking. Two lines form on the east side of the room, by the big windows. I get up, cane in hand, and slowly move in that direction. I feel wobbly. Before I know it, one of the women grabs a folding chair, takes it to the side of the room, and offers it to me. I readily accept and sit down.

Watching and listening, I see every student start with legs parallel, hip-width apart.

"Sink all your weight into your left leg; now pick up your right foot, take a small step forward, heel first, then foot. Now shift your weight onto the right leg. Pick up your left foot, step forward, keeping hip-width and parallel, heel first, then your foot." I continue to watch while remaining seated. The walking practice is slow and it takes balance that I know I don't have.

Our teacher asks us to focus on the standing leg, the leg that has all the weight on it. She says it is important to be rooted like a tree, stand tall like a tree. It's the rooting on one leg that allows the flexibility to pick up the "free" leg and take a small step forward.

It's so slow. These people have been doing this for a while. They know what to do and seem so stable. My light bulb dims as I watch from my chair, knowing my balance is worse than anybody in the room.

As the class continues to walk, the teacher comes over to me, suggests I try this walking by supporting myself with my hand on the wall. I stand up, grab my cane, and walk with her to the south wall of the room. She places her left hand against the wall and slowly starts to walk. I stand behind her and try to follow. This is hard. My legs are wobbly and I'm afraid of falling when trying to balance on one leg. I believe her that keeping good alignment and hip-width distance between my legs are what might help me walk better, but right now I can only do that with an aide, the wall. My hand stays flush against the wall and I'm able to take ten steps forward. Then I need to sit down. I'm glad all these people in class are strangers because that makes me feel less self-conscious.

The class ends. I feel exhausted and somewhat deflated because I don't feel like I could do much of the class. Two women come over to see me, introduce themselves, and comment that they hope I liked the class and might come back again next week. That makes me feel better. They're kind and understanding, like my mother.

I leave the building and walk slowly, crossing Michigan Avenue to catch a bus home. While waiting for the bus, I reflect on my experience: not one thing in class was familiar; I couldn't do much; the teacher and students were very nice and welcoming. But I'm tired and discouraged that my body isn't strong enough to participate fully.

I give myself a pep talk. *You have to start where you are, Arlene.* At least I can get to class, follow the teacher from a chair, and use the wall to aid in walking. At least I'm off my couch. By the time I arrive home, I've done an about-face with my attitude. In my head, I hear my mother saying not to dwell on what my body can't do. I'll take her good advice. I want to be like these seniors when I am their age—vibrant and full of energy.

I will return.

CHAPTER 43

Roller Coaster

The next day, in the narrow hallway between my living room and bedroom, I stand and place my left palm on the left wall and right palm against the right wall at shoulder level. *Relax, Arlene. Relax your shoulders.*

With my hands in position, I look down to see if my feet are parallel, hip-width apart. I take a breath in, put all the weight on my left foot, and raise my right leg and foot. My leg feels heavy. I can only lift it a couple of inches off the floor. I place my heel down, then my foot, then shift my weight to that foot. The wall keeps me balanced. Facing straight ahead, slowly, methodically, I practice the Tai Chi walk. *Remember, the tortoise wins, not the hare.* That is me, a tortoise in training. A smile fills my face.

I reach the end of the seven-foot-long hallway, like a marathon runner reaching the finish line with focus and determination. It took about ten minutes. *Victory! I made it.* I'm proud of myself.

◆ ◆ ◆

The next week I'm in Nancy's treatment room. "You're warm, Arlene. I can feel your Qi is scattered," Nancy says. "I sense some anxiety, so we'll work on channels and acupuncture points to help bring calmness."

"I'm not used to this, Nancy. Usually I'm even-keeled, but in the last few weeks my emotions have been up and down and I'm not sleeping well. I start reading a novel and can't focus. I walk into my bedroom and am not sure what I'm doing there. My eyes tear up for no reason. I don't understand what's going on. I'm seeing you and taking Tai Chi class, so I should be calmer."

Nancy reassures me that even though I'm doing good things for my body, it's a lot of change for me, which can be unsettling. She starts talking about my body.

"We can see our body as an enemy and we can see our body as a friend. It's not either-or. Most of us see some positives and some negatives but have a dominant view of our body as a positive or negative. Where are you?" she asks me.

I look down, collect my thoughts. "Give me a few seconds to think about this." *My mind is blank.*

Silence. Nancy does not jump in to fill the void. She waits, gives me time.

Lifting my head to look at her, I say, "Off the top of my head, I think my attitude toward my body is positive. Looking back, I've always thought my body proportions and weight have been a plus for me. I've been good at sports, like basketball and baseball. I exercise, eat well, am fit. But . . ."

"But what, Arlene? Go on."

"Since my early twenties, when I lost all feeling from my waist down, I've struggled with pain and numbness, capped off by difficulty in walking. For twenty-six years I haven't known if my body would be strong or not. I still can't count on it to work properly."

"So, you feel like your body has let you down?" Nancy asks.

"Yes, I do," I say, my voice loud and sharp. "Oh my," I say, catching myself in a moment of anger, "listen to how I sound. I'm surprising myself."

"That's okay," Nancy reassures me. "Your body wants attention, caring. You're paying attention and are open to helping your body heal. We're working together. You're regularly doing Tai Chi. These are good things. It takes time and it takes patience."

This discussion with Nancy energizes me. It's May, spring has arrived, and the sun is shining. I've been seeing Nancy for nine months and have been doing Tai Chi for over a month. I have a heightened sense of alertness, balance, and being. I'm on a high. Part of that may be the release of tension I feel by admitting my body has disappointed me. Nancy said it's okay. Keep going.

A month later, I feel the opposite, tired, dragging, off-balance, aching legs. I'm on a roller coaster. How can I make sense of such highs and lows—one moment exciting, the next moment confusing?

I keep at it. Glimpses of heightened energy and moments of more normal mobility outweigh the setbacks. Seeing possibilities motivates me. I now understand what Nancy means about being a partner with her. On her treatment table, I'm ready and open the minute we start.

It helps that I now talk to my body, letting it know I'm listening and it's my priority. I pay attention to what it's telling me and quiet my mind when it tells me to push through its limits.

One night, I'm reading *Journey to the Heart*, a book of daily meditations by Melody Beattie, and see this:[1]

---

1   Melody Beattie, *Journey to the Heart: Daily Meditations on the Path to Freeing Your Soul* (New York: HarperCollins, 1996).

Our bodies can help provide us with direction. Many of us have heard the expression I'm leaning toward that or I'm leaning away from that. When we're centered and balanced, our body will help show us what we really want to do. We will literally lean toward or away from what we like or don't like. We've spent much of our lives forcing our body into situations, into energy fields and circumstances that it leaned away from, resisted, or moved back from. Then we wondered why we hurt and felt uncomfortable.

The more we honor our body, the more it will help lead us. And the more it will become a natural guide helping us on our path, reflecting the desires of our heart and soul. The more we learn to trust our body, the more we'll come into harmony with our natural rhythms, the cycles, and movements of our lives.

That is profound. I read it again.

She reinforces what I am trying to learn, to trust my body more. I feel better about my body. What I didn't expect is the emotional aspect that has been unleashed through this bodywork. I'm on a high, have an *a-ha moment*, then sink low, discouraged, wondering if this effort is worth it. *I must learn to accept what is. It's hard.* My body is teaching me patience. It's healing at its own pace. But my head still wants to move ahead of my body.

As autumn leaves start to change colors, I'm more stable and fluid with my Tai Chi. I stand, step out, step back, and shift my weight through the gentle, flowing movements. I can make it through most classes without the need to sit. Most days, I can be up four to five hours before needing to lie down and rest. The goal Nancy suggested, changing my pattern of one-step-forward-two-backward to two-forward-then-one-backward, has become a reality. *Can I go more steps forward?*

CHAPTER 44

You Have to Take Your Body with You

I tell Mom about reaching my goal of moving to two steps forward, one backward. "I'm glad to hear you like Tai Chi so much," Mom says over the phone, always reassuring, happy for my victories. "You sound more energetic and enthusiastic than you have in a long time."

"Yes, Mom, I'm making progress." I hesitate for a moment. "Wow, did you hear what I just said? I *am* making progress. That's the first time I've felt that in my body for over twenty-six years. I'm so excited!"

A week later, I ride the bus down to the Art Institute of Chicago, excited to see an Edgar Degas exhibit that's recently opened. I rent the audio tour and walk around unaided throughout the galleries. A little more than an hour later, I finish and make my way out of the gallery. I suddenly stop, head feeling foggy and fatigue starting to descend into my body. *Fresh air. I need fresh air.* I get myself outside, use the railing to get down the steps to the Michigan Avenue sidewalk.

I don't know if I can get one foot in front of the other. I feel overwhelmed, so fatigued I can't think. I want to lie down on the sidewalk. I don't care what it looks like. Somehow, I have enough presence to hail a cab and get myself home. Once inside my apartment, I lie down on the floor. My body feels like a dead weight. It takes about twenty minutes before I get my body upright and make my way to the couch.

I lie still and focus on breathing to clear my mind. This sudden fatigue has caught me by surprise. I'm confounded about what just happened because I saw Nancy yesterday. She was excited because, as she said, my energy channels are open and moving well. Sigh. I'm sick of these sudden downturns. Will my life ever return to normal? Normal? I haven't used that word for years because I don't know what normal is for me.

My mind keeps active, even as my body feels like a dead weight. It was a year ago when I started seeing Nancy. I was up one day, then down the following two. I'm better a year later. It's always been slow and I can't expect a complete turnaround in one year. It's not linear—it zigs and zags, goes up and down. I'm rationalizing. I've been punched in the stomach, fallen to the floor, been thrown back to discouragement.

Based on this jolting setback, I schedule an appointment with Nancy for the following week.

♦ ♦ ♦

"Hi, Arlene." I hear that reassuring, comforting voice as the office door opens into the waiting room.

"Your shirt is great, Arlene. I like the deep purple color with all those multicolored rectangles and hearts on it. You're changing your clothing style, aren't you?"

"Yes. I want more patterns, more color, and looser fitting clothes. I found a brand that seems to fit where I want to go."

Sitting in the familiar chair facing Nancy, I say, "This past Friday was awful. I don't know why I had such a dip downward the day after my appointment with you. Am I really making progress? How can I reduce the extreme fluctuations?"

"You are making progress, Arlene," Nancy says. "You are much more tuned into your body. You are listening to it." Nancy points out my progress with walking, with Tai Chi, and being able to have longer periods of activity before having to lie down and rest.

"I need that reminder. It's so easy to have doubts and fears creep in and take over."

Nancy's reassurance keeps me going. She's my anchor in the uncertainty that faces me every day.

◆ ◆ ◆

After that appointment I rebound. My energy seems to level off. It's September and I continue my walking and energy ball practice every day at home and Tai Chi with seniors once a week. My teacher asks me to lead the class when she's not there. I've let go of doing the Tai Chi form perfectly and it's serving me well. I know the moves and feel confident leading the class when my teacher asks. I sign up for a public class she teaches in Lincoln Park. I lie down for at least two hours every day. Some days my legs ache; some days they don't. My life isn't a roller coaster right now. It's more like riding gentle waves in the ocean.

I have less cosmic anxiety—the old feeling that *everything is going so well, so when will the shoe drop, when will the bottom fall out* has lessened. I'm learning to be patient. I have to because progress is so slow. For so long now, *improvement* has not meant to add something; it's meant a lessening of something that already exists: less aching, less fatigue. *The tortoise wins*, I remind myself again. On the plus side, I have longer periods of sustained energy that motivate me to keep going. Amy checks in with me at least twice a week. She continues to reinforce what I'm doing and encourages me to keep going, regardless of how slow it is.

♦ ♦ ♦

A few months later, in March 1997, my thoughts drift to what I'm going to do next, what I'm going to do to make a contribution, to be productive. I talk to the owner of a local bookstore about a part-time job. She has nothing available, which is probably a good thing. I don't know what kind of hours I could commit to and have confidence my body will cooperate.

In Nancy's office for my regular appointment, she asks how my body is feeling.

"I'm frustrated."

"Why? What's going on?" she says.

"I'm feeling better now, can be up doing things for longer periods of time. I want to do something, maybe work part-time." I move up to the edge of my chair, facing Nancy. "But my body doesn't allow me to plan even a day in advance. When I wake up in the morning, I don't know how long my body can be upright and moving. I don't know what to do."

Nancy hesitates for a few seconds, tuned into my words and my anxiety. Then she says, "Whatever you do, you have to take your body with you."

I stare at Nancy. Nothing comes out of my mouth. Abruptly, I stand. *She should understand me. I feel resistance. How much should I push?*

"I don't want to do that, Nancy," I say, with conviction. "My body isn't reliable from day to day. I want to do something that's not dependent on my body."

"Take your time, Arlene. You have come so far. Your body is your friend. Your body can help direct you to what is next." *My body doesn't feel like my friend.*

"I know I'm totally in my head right now. This got me into trouble before. I need to reconnect with my body."

But how?

— CHAPTER 45 —

On the Road Again

I deas about what to do next aren't streaming into my head. That doesn't stop me from taking advantage of my sustained energy. In late spring of 1997, I rendezvous with my Heavenly Seven college friends in Brooklyn. They are so excited that I'm stable and have energy to get on an airplane. Their enduring friendships anchor me and we laugh often when we're together. I pace myself by doing one activity a day and resting often.

A month after Brooklyn I travel to Paris, Brussels, and Holland with Carol and Stacy. They plan their day and I join them for one activity. The hour I spend at the Musée d'Orsay thrills me. I feel stable and energetic, able to make plans and keep them.

In early summer, Mom calls. "I want to throw out something to you. I've been thinking about going to San Diego for a few weeks, to get away this winter. Since Carol lives there, she can help scout out a place, maybe close to the ocean. Think about hearing those ocean waves lapping up on the shore. Do you think you could go too? The milder temperatures might be good for you."

"Mom, that sounds wonderful," I say, already seeing myself doing Tai Chi under a palm tree. "It could be lots of fun."

◆ ◆ ◆

Mom gets right on it and secures a rental apartment in San Diego for early November. She suggests I stay longer and get my own little apartment. On November 1, I meet Mom at O'Hare and we board a United flight to San Diego, my winter home for the next four months. Mom will stay for six weeks and I'm so glad we'll have that time together. Carol meets us at the airport. It's 74 degrees and a cloudless, blue sky welcomes us. We shed our winter coats and take off north to Carlsbad.

After exiting Carlsbad Village Drive, we go a mile or so west, until we can go no farther—Ocean Street, aptly named because the Pacific Ocean is right there. We park, get out, and gaze at the expansive water in front of us, shimmering in the bright afternoon sun. A few surfers in black wetsuits do their thing, ride the waves, look for more waves.

"Hope we can see some dolphins while we're here," I say to Mom and Carol.

"Me too," Mom says. "Maybe we'll see them from my balcony. I just love this soft air."

◆ ◆ ◆

My stand-alone, one-bedroom apartment is part of the Ocean Palms Beach Resort, a quaint amalgam of apartments and a small hotel.

Not fancy, but not beachy either. Mom has a large one-bedroom apartment, with a huge living room and a balcony that looks directly out on the beach and ocean. It's only a half block from my cozy apartment. Every morning we walk together on the boardwalk that abuts the ocean. Our pace is leisurely and we take time to stop and watch the surfers riding the Pacific Ocean waves. I'm walking normally without my cane.

My priorities right now are to walk with Mom every day and find a Tai Chi class. I learn that the Pacific School of Tai Chi in Solana Beach teaches the same Yang style developed by Cheng Man-ch'ing that I'm learning in Chicago.

I join a class at the Pacific School, which is a half-hour bus ride. The second-floor room is about half the size of a gymnasium with twenty to twenty-five people warming up when I walk in.

The teacher, Chris, is a very tall, blond-haired man. He takes his position in the middle of the room as class begins and says that four senior trainers anchor the class, one at each corner. They will set the speed of our movements, so regardless of which direction you are facing, watch one of them. *Well, that takes the pressure off. I won't stick out.*

I learn that a course on the history and origins of Tai Chi is to be offered at the Taoist Sanctuary, taught by a Taoist priest named Ted. Curious about this subject, I sign up.

"Tai Chi emanates from Taoism," Ted says the first night. "Taoism is the Way and follows nature, the natural order of the universe." One evening he makes a statement that jolts me. Standing at a blackboard, he writes "wander aimlessly" on the board with his white chalk. "This is what we want to learn to do, focus on the moment, be open with no fixed destination."

That is so different from what I've focused on most of my life. Before working with Nancy, I placed my attention on achieving goals. But now, focusing on the moment makes sense to me. Boy, has my view of the world been turned upside down. I'm not striving to reach goals, always on the go. Tai Chi helps me create stillness, be in the moment, and be comfortable with it. Plus, it feels so good to not make to-do lists anymore. From now on, I will focus on the moment without a fixed destination.

— CHAPTER 46 —

The Close

My four months in San Diego pass quickly. I return to Chicago and rejoin my fellow Tai Chi students. We're learning the *close* of our Tai Chi form, which is the last move. The form is a sequence of moves to balance yin and yang. Right now, two of us at a time have to do the form in front of the rest of the class. I go to the center of the room for my turn, look at my partner, and in unison we say, "Preparation," which starts us moving. I focus on one step after another, trying to move from my waist and hips, shifting my weight in a smooth, slow manner. My balance is stable, allowing me to step out with ease. I'm not nervous. These are familiar moves and it doesn't make any difference if I'm not the most balanced or graceful person in the room. Tai Chi has helped me let go of all that.

Once we've all had a chance to do our form, my teacher says, "Now the hard work and fun begin. We'll work to really relax and feel our Qi more. But let's take this moment to congratulate our-selves on a big moment, knowing all the moves of the form." I'm elated to be at this point; it's something I couldn't have imagined a couple of years ago. How far I've come from that first day I walked with my cane into a Tai Chi class with seniors.

◆ ◆ ◆

Three months later in June, I'm on Nancy's treatment table. I have a big a-ha moment. My body feels alive. As Nancy's hands move across my back and my skin, I feel an evenness of the touch. My legs don't ache and strength in my leg muscles has increased. I'm alert, with a sharp mind. The a-ha comes as I realize this is the manifestation of what Nancy has repeatedly emphasized, "It's a process." It's my daily discipline of Tai Chi, working every other week with Nancy, eating nutritious food, and perhaps the four months of even temperatures in San Diego that are all paying off.

I feel a harmony in my body and spirit. I'm at a place of living in my body that is greater than I've ever experienced. I'm not taking any medication. My Qi is moving more freely. Nancy comments that she doesn't feel the blockages I once had. She feels openness. I do too. It's a freeing feeling. *Thank you, body, for being patient, for giving my mind a chance to slow down and catch up.*

◆ ◆ ◆

Two months later, I'm with Nancy in her office.

"I have really exciting news, Arlene," she says with a huge smile. I feel her excitement and anticipation. "I'm going to open a holistic health center in downtown Evanston next year."

"Fantastic, Nancy, tell me more."

She talks about bringing together a group of professional health-care practitioners, acupuncturists, psychotherapists, massage therapists, and physical therapists. She glances at me and pauses.

"And I want to have Tai Chi classes in my center. Isn't that exciting?"

"Yes, very exciting!" Without missing a beat, I continue, "I'll talk to my teacher to see if she has time and will come to Evanston. I hope so."

"No, Arlene. I want you to teach. I want your energy here," Nancy replies, with certainty and without hesitation.

I freeze, stunned. *Me? While I've made so much progress personally, it's a huge responsibility to lead others in their journeys. It feels daunting. Am I really ready? Do I have what it takes?*

"Oh, Nancy, I have to think about this. I feel honored that you want me to teach. Thank you, but I don't know if I am ready."

Nancy looks confidently at me with a smile. "You are ready, Arlene. You are ready."

CHAPTER 47

Class Begins

A year later in September 1999, Nancy opens her holistic health center, Heartwood, in downtown Evanston, on the second floor of a building across the street from Bennison's Bakery.

I have said yes to Nancy's offer. She probably knows my body and readiness better than I do, but I am listening to my body, learning from it. For most of my life I've analyzed, considered options carefully, then made a decision, but not with Nancy. I took a leap into the unknown with her. I trusted Amy's experience. Now I'm trusting Nancy and going for it.

With excitement and anticipation, like shopping with Mom for school supplies before my first day of junior high, I spend hours preparing for this class: sequencing the moves, writing down the warm-ups (part of the Eight Pieces of Silk Brocade), Tai Chi walking, then introducing Preparation and Beginning, the first two moves of the form. Besides lesson plans for my first week of class, I buy clothes for teaching: two pairs of black, drawstring cotton pants with a slightly flared leg and low-cut tie shoes, gray with three maroon stripes on each side. *Boy*, I think, *this is a complete makeover, a new beginning. I'm so glad I'm not out buying a tailored gray jacket and skirt. That was then. This is now.*

On the first Wednesday in October, I approach the front door, about to teach my first Tai Chi class. *Click.* I turn the brass knob and open the door. Green, carpeted steps face me. Steep steps, fourteen of them. I shudder, suddenly feeling overwhelmed. *Can I do this? Can I climb all those steps? Wait a minute. I don't need to feel those steps are an impossible mountain to climb.* They are old tapes in my head about an old nemesis. Grasping the handrail with my left hand, I methodically conquer each of the fourteen steps without questioning myself.

♦ ♦ ♦

I walk into the room where I'll teach my first Tai Chi class. *My* class. When I entered my first class three years ago with my cane and sat on the chair, I never would have imagined I could someday lead my own class. It's sinking in that it's real.

Twenty minutes later, three students stand in the classroom.

"Welcome. Let's introduce ourselves and say what we hope to get from the class."

April, tall, slender, with short black spiked hair, speaks up. She says she has no cartilage in her right ankle. It's throwing off her balance, so she is after better balance. Katherine, tall and big-boned, with light brown shoulder-length hair, says she had back surgery about a year ago. She had bones fused together, resulting in difficulty turning from side to side, bending forward, and climbing steps. She wants to increase her range of motion and flexibility. Lynn is tiny, with short, blond hair. She's in her midforties and wants to learn how to relax more, slow down.

I take a deep breath. I've led my teacher's class many times, but this is my class. I want it to be good for the students. "I want your energy here," Nancy's voice whispers in my head. I don't have any written notes. I did detailed preparation, but today I've left my lesson plans at home on purpose. If I veer from my plan, fine. If I only focus on breathing and walking, fine.

I start the class. "Tai Chi originated in China centuries ago. The goal is balance in all things, starting with our own bodies. The slow, flowing movements follow the rhythms of nature and help us be in the moment. Now let's bring our attention to our bodies, with our legs and feet parallel, about hip-width apart," I say and demonstrate. My legs feel strong today. I let go of any doubts about doing a good job. Tai Chi teaches to go with the flow, so that's where I want to be.

Lynn looks down at her feet. April shakes out her shoulders and arms, looking squarely at me.

"Breathe in. And out. Again. Inhale. And exhale." *This feels so right, just going with the flow. These women are with me.*

Nancy was right. I am ready.

— CHAPTER 48 —

The Canadian Bluebird

The next week in my appointment with Nancy, I excitedly talk about my first class and what a privilege it is to teach Tai Chi. My attention quickly shifts to my body. "My hot flashes are very intense. When I opened my refrigerator last night, I wanted to crawl in and stay for a while," I say to Nancy, half kidding, but with a touch of desperation.

Nancy smiles but knows this is serious business. "Your hot flashes rival the worst I have felt," Nancy says. "We'll work today on reducing some of that heat."

While I'm on the massage table, Nancy presses points on my back with her hands, starting from my tailbone up to the back of my neck. Even with the aching hands, cold fingers, and hot flashes on my forehead, Nancy comments that my meridians are open, including my heart meridian.

"Where do you see that I am right now, Nancy?" I say, a little muffled because my mouth is smashed into the face cradle.

"Your legs are strong, particularly your quadriceps. That's your Tai Chi working. You have built up your Qi base. Really, Arlene, you're doing so well at your essence."

As Nancy continues to press points on my body and use her elbows and fists to massage tight areas, I feel heat pour out the bottom of my feet. When I first started seeing Nancy, progress was slow in her treatment room. I didn't feel much change for a long while. As she helped me get in touch with my body and worked with me as a partner, changes sped up. Never would I have felt heat pour from my feet so quickly a year ago.

"Can you put a light blanket over me, Nancy?" I'm not only getting rid of the heat, but I'm feeling a little chilled as well. What a difference I feel, and so quickly.

Head still facing down, I feel a tiny smile forming on my face. *How far I have come.*

◆ ◆ ◆

I tell Nancy I'm curious to learn more about energy, about the principles of Tai Chi and how they relate to Chinese medicine, which she explains gets to the root cause of a health issue and not just the symptoms.

I decide I want to study Chinese medicine.

I apply and am accepted into the Pacific College of Oriental Medicine, a new Chicago branch of the school headquartered in San Diego. I enroll in master's level classes to focus on fundamentals and understand terminology. I don't intend to commit to a four-year degree program but want to learn how the fundamentals of Chinese medicine relate to Tai Chi and the flow of Qi. Nancy talks often about Qi, as does my Tai Chi teacher. Now I do, too, and am eager to know more about how Qi relates to a healthy body and mind.

And maybe someday I can go to China, to study, to experience Qi at the source of this system of medicine and Tai Chi. For now, that's only a dream because I don't have the stamina and strength to take such a big trip.

I'm excited about this intellectual pursuit and am aware once again of my seismic shift, the reversal of my pattern throughout most of my life. I jumped into experiencing Nancy without exhaustive research and I'm doing the same with my academic studies. I trusted Amy's experience. I've learned to listen to my body and walk in partnership with Nancy. Now I'm ready to put my head into it at Pacific College.

♦ ♦ ♦

I feel what Nancy reaffirms for me, more sustained energy. I don't hesitate to go with Mom on a train adventure. We ride the Rocky Mountaineer train across the Canadian Rockies: Calgary, Banff, and Vancouver. We start with snow-capped mountains jutting up against the blue sky in Banff. We have a spectacular view of a mountain peak right outside our hotel window. What a great place to be in 2000 as the new millennium unfolds.

I want to listen to my body and not run myself down. I decide to forgo the six-hour group bus tour out of Banff to Lake Louise, and choose to rest and do some Tai Chi in a downtown park near the river.

On a large green lawn by a big tree, I practice Tai Chi. A group of four- and five-year-olds run, playing a game and giggling. About thirty yards away on the grass are two brilliant bluebirds (larger than those in the States). I turn to my left, face the river, take in a deep breath, and lift my arms in front of me. As I exhale, I bring my arms down to the center of my body. A slight breeze drifts across my shoulders. I breathe in the fresh, clean air.

Stepping around into single whip, I shift my weight forward on my left leg. I stop at what I see. No more than six feet directly in front of me on the ground is a bluebird, watching me. I had been told these bluebirds in Canada are more aggressive and standoffish than those in the States. I stay motionless in the single whip position. I don't want to cause the bird to move. When I can hold this stance no longer, I pick up my back leg to stand in parallel. The bird flies away. I revel in my mind about what just happened—that bird felt my Tai Chi energy connected with nature and was attracted to it, to me. The tall tree with deep roots, the bright green grass, the meandering river, the bluebird, and me coalesced. We were all in harmony and connected.

CHAPTER 49

Being Teacher

Three months after the trip across the Canadian Rockies, I begin teaching my first evening Tai Chi class. I have four students in this class, dealing with various physical and psychological issues—anxiety, depression, arthritis. They want to slow down and get more focus. One woman in her early forties works in a medical organization dealing with all kinds of cardiac issues. She feels so much pressure and works many hours at high speed. She's afraid of burnout and her "head exploding."

"Only do what you can do," I say, facing the four students as class starts. "We all look perfectly fine on the outside, but we all have issues we're dealing with."

I ask the students to frame their fingers over their dan tien (lower abdomen) and breathe. "I really only have two expectations for class. First, listen to your body and don't do anything that's uncomfortable, and second, try to keep your mind in the room."

I have their attention. With feet parallel, hip-width apart, we shift our weight to the balls of our feet, back to center, on the outside of the feet, on the instep, back to center. "Now, move around, in small circles or side to side, visualizing your feet like the trunk of a tree, sprouting roots deep into the earth. The deeper our roots go, the more balanced and centered we will be."

Fifteen minutes quickly pass. We practice the Tai Chi walk with focus on the standing leg. "We focus on where we are right now, on the rooted leg. It's not important where we're going. Regardless of our starting point, we can all improve our walking, starting with being mindful, paying attention." I'm telling my students and myself the very things that my teachers told me back in my early Tai Chi days to help me keep going.

I start to think, could Tai Chi be something bigger? Could it be a business of sorts for me? But not like my days at United. I imagine I would teach three or four classes a week, market my classes to attract students, and then share with them the moves and energy of Tai Chi that continue to be so helpful to me. A woman in my Tuesday evening class is a marketing professional and website designer. We start talking about developing a website and a business card. My niece Stacy, also a creative marketing and design person, starts preparing a logo for me. I want a unique, stylized yin-yang symbol, just for me.

My business experience, including serving on boards of Planned Parenthood/Illinois and the Fourth Presbyterian Church of Chicago, serve me well with Tai Chi. Maybe I'll build a business, one step at a time. No rush. I don't feel driven, don't feel any *shoulds*. I like thinking about possibilities. My business mind is active, so I have to remind myself that the tortoise wins, to keep perspective and live in the moment.

♦ ♦ ♦

Teaching two Tai Chi classes, as well as being a student in another, increases my stamina, strength, and flexibility. My moves are more fluid. It's September 2001 and Mom and I plan to go on a cruise. Then terrorists strike on September 11. We delay our trip for a year: In the fall of 2002, we sail on a fourteen-day cruise through the Panama Canal. I'm so glad I opened up to Mom all those years ago because it's allowed us to take all these trips together. If I hadn't told her about my MS, I would have been worried what to say if I needed to rest or had a spell. Now I am open and Mom can see all of me.

For my church, I take on a new volunteer activity. I join a team of teachers, leading classes on church history, theology, and governance to prospective new members. On a spring evening in 2003, I arrive home after the class and face an envelope in my mailbox from United. My shoulders tense up, sensing something ominous inside.

The letter is less than one page. In formal, legalese language, it says the company has undertaken a review of personnel policies. This letter specifically relates to changes in the long-term disability (LTD) policy for management. The policy is being capped at three years. For those employees who have been on LTD for more than three years, they will be terminated or can retire, if eligible. Two options. Blunt. Final.

My heart sinks. *Terminated. I'm going to be terminated. What about my medical coverage? What if my savings runs out? My Tai Chi teaching may end because I can't make enough money to live on. Will I relapse and need my cane to stand and walk?* This is the worst. I'm uninsurable. I go to the kitchen, pour a glass of wine.

Back on my living room couch, I reread the letter. The first time, I blanked out after seeing the word *terminated*. This time I focus on the last sentence, and it changes everything: "Effective date, May 1, 2003." My birthday. It will be my fifty-fifth birthday and I will qualify for early retirement. I can continue my medical coverage! Oh, my heavens, I can't believe this. It's serendipity or a miracle! What are the odds that the very day the policy takes effect is my birthday? I'm so excited and take a moment to say thank you, God. *Thank you, universe.*

— CHAPTER 50 —

Life Calling

A year passes and my classes continue through 2004. As students tell me their stories, I wonder if I should tell them about my zigzag entrance into Tai Chi and my struggle to keep going. But what will they think if only a few years ago I used a cane and sat in a chair throughout class? Will they think I'm not experienced enough to be their teacher?

I'm inspired by the courage of my students. Beth tells me about her challenges. She is self-conscious about her hands with limited dexterity from decades of the ravages of rheumatoid arthritis. She thinks the first thing people notice is her hands, but the first thing I notice is her fluidity and graceful movement. I tell her that. She's hard on herself, expecting a lot.

I admire Beth's strength and determination in facing her challenges. She sees multiple doctors, stays open to healthy practices, and rarely misses a Tai Chi class. She embodies the slow flowing moves of Tai Chi and often mentions how they help manage her pain, clear her head, and help her balance. Currently she is fatigued, going through multiple tests for new symptoms that indicate she might have lupus. I feel a kindred spirit with her, and even though I don't have her specific chronic conditions, I do identify because I know about the uncertainty, the surprises that a chronic condition can thrust upon a person. I love Beth's presence in the classroom. She exudes positive, can-do energy.

Kathy shares her story with me. The first thing she says in class when I ask what she hopes to gain from Tai Chi is "All I want to do is to be able to pick up a dinner plate from the kitchen cabinet, put dishes in the dishwasher, and carry groceries." She had to stop working due to pain from rheumatoid arthritis and an interconnective tissue disorder. Although she's just in her forties, her daily activities are severely compromised. She walks into the classroom slowly, with almost wooden-like movements. Her fingers on both hands are semifrozen, with little ability to move her knuckle joints.

She has an endearing smile and is a little playful. After about twenty minutes of standing in class, she has to sit down and be still. I affirm her decision to take breaks, to just be. Kathy is a good example of someone listening to her body, doing only what she can. She does her research and has excellent medical doctors, a gifted acupuncturist, and now Tai Chi.

♦ ♦ ♦

I decide to tell my story because it might be helpful for students to stick with Tai Chi. "I'm a really good poster child for Tai Chi," I tell my Thursday morning class. "I can only speak for myself," I add, walking slowly back and forth in front of the seven students facing me. "Tai Chi has helped me regain my ability to walk. That's given me a lot of passion for a regular walking practice."

When I start sharing, my students are amazed.

"I'm so inspired by your story," Beth says. "I like coming here. You're so patient and gentle in telling us to take this time not to judge ourselves. You are a role model for patience. I like that because I need that reminder often."

"Tai Chi is not about trying harder. It's about letting go. Arlene, I hear you saying that, even when I'm outside of class," Kathy says as we take a short break. With a big smile on her face, she adds, "I sometimes catch myself trying harder to let go." Everybody laughs. That hits home for most of us.

"Isn't it good to not take ourselves so seriously?" I add. It's even calming to pay attention to the language we use. Rather than using aggressive, military-type words, we switch to phrases like *ward off* rather than *fight off*. Rather than *battle* the illness or *conquer* toe disease, in Chinese medicine and Tai Chi we use words like *build*, *replenish* the Qi, and *fortify* our natural body defenses. I love my students. We're building community class by class. When I'm open, it gives my students permission to be the same.

"Isn't it exciting when focusing our attention on the standing leg as we walk is our biggest accomplishment of the day?" I say to the class. "If you say that at home, you might get a weird look from your family members. But here, we all understand and can feel really good about it." Heads nod up and down.

I'm humbled and warmed by comments from students: "I'm sleeping better." "My pain decreases immeasurably during class." "I'm more aware of my walking, less afraid that I'll fall."

◆ ◆ ◆

Driving home, I reflect. I seem to get regular comments about how patient and calm I am as a teacher, that my voice is steady and comforting. I feel so honored to be able to pass on a centuries-old wisdom and practice that has been, and continues to be, so helpful to me. Incorporating principles and gentle movements into my days has transformed my life. And now it's doing that for my students.

I've found my life calling and I'm taking my body with me.

— CHAPTER 51 —

Earth Energy

Tai Chi is an integral part of my daily life, like eating breakfast and brushing my teeth. Every day I strive to get stronger
and improve my balance. It's not unusual for someone to
ask "Are you in remission?" or "Are you cured?" I usually say that I'm
not sure, but what I know is that my health continues to improve
every day. I'm so much healthier in my fifties than I was in my twenties and thirties.

As my stamina improves, I seek out Tai Chi workshops and
opportunities to learn from great teachers. I have loved my diversity
of Tai Chi experiences in San Diego. Now that I can safely plan to
travel, knowing I am strong enough, I do. In 2004, just a month after
receiving that letter from United, I fly to Santa Rosa, California, for
a weekend to get certified in a Tai Chi program. Although just two
days of training, I need to lie down after the morning break for forty-
five minutes and also in midafternoon. I don't sleep but stretch my

body out to be still and replenish my energy. I inform my teacher about my condition in advance and she's very understanding.

Two years later, in 2006, when I need to recertify, I attend a training session in the San Diego area and meet the teacher, Troyce. I connect with her. Her teaching makes me feel calm and alive. About five feet tall with long, blond hair pulled back into a ponytail, she is rooted, as graceful as a ballet dancer, and strong. I think she could easily hold her own against a three-hundred-pound man.

Troyce is conducting a workshop in Bend, Oregon, in August 2006 and invites me to come. I'm excited to study with her and also to see Bend, which I've heard is a beautiful area.

Troyce is leading an in-depth Tai Chi workshop for kids and teenagers, in a dance studio equipped with mirrors and ballet bars. We are all experienced Tai Chi teachers who know the same form. Troyce focuses on deepening the moves, on feeling different levels of energy.

"It is called *peng jing* energy," Troyce explains, "the energy that comes up through enacting a string of pearls, that energy force starting from below the ground, earth energy moving up through the feet, leading from the waist, flowering through the hands." As Troyce talks about this energy, she moves her body into a single whip, demonstrating in action what she is saying. I see a tiny lift, for just a second, in her body. I aspire to that grace I see before me, like a ballet dancer suspended for just a moment in the air.

In the afternoon, twenty of us anticipate doing a familiar Tai Chi form. There is openness in the room, like an empty jar, lid off, ready to be filled.

"Settle your energy in the tan t'ien. Feel a helium balloon at the center top of your head, gently pulling you up," Troyce says. "Focus on the force field, bringing up earth energy into your body. Begin."

A warm sensation moves up my legs. We all shift weight to our right leg, step forward with the left, shifting all weight to that leg. Dark brown hair, blond hair, slim, pudgy, tall, short—we are all moving together as one. Twenty left legs step forward in unison. We are collective breath, one unit with many arms and legs, like a well-choreographed ballet. Time stops. My body remembers and flows, knowing what move comes next. A feeling of complete serenity and peacefulness envelops me. I'm in the present moment like I've never before experienced.

The Tai Chi experience in Bend is, well, magical. Besides the Tai Chi a-ha, I reach a huge milestone. This is the first time I make it through a two-day workshop without having to lie down! My stamina is increased and the collective energy of Troyce and the Tai Chi colleagues I'm with carry me forward. I've climbed to a new plateau and my Tai Chi and work with Nancy are key to getting me to this point.

— CHAPTER 52 —

Stories

I'm excited to share my Bend experience with my students and work with them to bring up earth energy from beneath their feet. It's a paradigm shift of what energy is, that energy has movement and power in itself. We imagine we're trees, tapping into the source of energy beneath the earth, moving it up and through our bodies. This image clicks with my students, and class by class, I see their slow, steady progress. There's more fluidity, flexibility, calm.

Then this week, Kathy walks into the Heartwood classroom with a big smile. Something is up. She says she's excited to share some big news with the class. Once everyone is in the room, she announces that the previous evening she took dinner plates out of the dishwasher and put them in the cupboard. She tells us it's Tai Chi and support from all of us that's gotten her to this point. We all clap, acknowledging this is a huge moment. With our own eyes we once saw Kathy's fingers frozen, and now they're moving, flexible,

functional. It's not from a pill or surgery but from the natural healing movements of Tai Chi that Kathy has totally embraced.

Then Beth speaks up. In her regular appointment with her
rheumatologist this week, he greeted her with a puzzled look. He
proceeded to tell her that her latest test results show decreased inflammation and he's going to lower the strength of her medicine. He says
he doesn't know what caused that, but he's pleased. She responded
to him with "Tai Chi." She has no doubts that her regular Tai Chi
practice is steadily bringing benefits, and this is such reinforcement.
Her doctor congratulates her and she's pleased he's so supportive of
her commitment to the practice.

I'm noticing that it's not just physical improvement for students
but mental and emotional as well. Denise is a great example. When
she initially called to inquire about Tai Chi, she mentioned her
beloved dog had just died and she needed something to center herself. Her veterinarian recommended Tai Chi, and although she liked
the idea, she didn't like group classes. I encouraged her to try one
class without a commitment to more.

Denise comes to a class and stands in the back corner of the
room. She is attentive to my instruction but tentative in moving her
body. She returns to the next class and keeps coming. She is quiet
and doesn't interact much with other students.

One evening after class, Denise asks if she can talk with me. She
tells me that every day she deals with anxiety and depression, which
are prevalent in her family. Her father lived with severe depression
and died by suicide. She lives with fear of worsening depression and
wants to learn how to manage it in a healthy way. This is a challenge
because she's not comfortable being in a group, talking about herself,
or joining a class. Her pattern has been to join a class and drop out

quickly or to ruminate about joining an exercise class but never take the step out the door to get herself to a classroom.

Denise feels comfortable in my Tai Chi class because it's an individual experience even in the midst of a group of people. She doesn't feel pressure to perform and finds my invitation to be where we are without expectations to be soothing. I watch her progress from being quiet, tentative, and shy to a place of confidence, better alignment, and ease of movement. She is disciplined and incorporates Tai Chi into her daily routine, when walking her dog, standing in line at the grocery store, or bicycling through the park.

The openness my students and I share, along with my study of Chinese medicine, makes me feel more integrated in my mind and body than I have ever experienced. It's a lightness of being, starting with a connection to earth energy.

— CHAPTER 53 —

Dad's Photos

Two years pass and I attend a second workshop with Troyce in Bend. Back in the Midwest, leaves are just starting to turn orange and brown and the slight chill in the air signals autumn will soon display its beautiful colors. The following weekend after returning from Bend, I drive to Mendota to visit Mom. It will be an extra fun weekend because my niece Stacy is also coming for a visit. I'm still on a high from the Bend experience and I know that spending time with Mom and Stacy will be good food for the soul as well.

Stacy and I both ask Mom to fix her fried chicken. My mouth waters thinking about it. It never disappoints. Right as we finish dinner on Saturday evening, Stacy starts talking about the World War II movies she's been watching. We kid her about her tendency to watch several movies at a time based in a time period, like those of Henry VIII and Queen Elizabeth. Right now, it's the period leading up and through World War II.

Always inquisitive, Stacy says, "Granddad told me stories about treating wounded soldiers on the frontlines in the war, how hard it was to see all the severe injuries and death. He also told me that he looked for his brother David and he named his son David after his brother. What's the story behind that?"

"I have an idea," Mom says. "Why don't we take a look at some of Dad's pictures? There's a picture of his brother David in his album."

"Dad's pictures?" Stacy and I say in unison. "I didn't know Dad had pictures," I add, feeling like our own family movie is about to unfold.

Mom walks to the hall closet and comes back into the kitchen with an album and a brown cardboard box. The large album is vintage style, with black leather front and back covers and no spine.

Mom, sitting between Stacy and me at the kitchen table, carefully opens the cover. I lean forward to see better. The thick black paper pages are covered with black-and-white photos from Dad's past.

"Have you seen all these pictures, Mom?" I ask, feeling a little nervous, wondering if there will be surprises. I know so little about Dad's past. I never thought about asking if Dad had pictures of his family and his time serving in the US Army.

"Yes, of course I have, but I haven't looked at them for many years," Mom answers matter-of-factly.

"Wow, Gram, I can't wait to see these," Stacy says, scooting her chair closer. "When I was a little girl, I remember Granddad talking about his family. Now I might get to see what they looked like."

On the first page are two pictures, one of a woman, one of a man, both posed, dressed up, looking right at the camera without a smile.

"This is your dad's mother, Rochel Falkowski, and his father, Mendel Falkowski, in 1937."

"Falkowski. That's the name Carol, David, and I saw on Dad's passport years ago. When did Dad change his name?" I ask.

"After he came to this country, he wanted a new start," Mom says. "He had his medical degree from the Sorbonne in Paris, but he had to complete residencies here to be licensed and practice medicine. It was not easy for a foreigner to fit in during the late 1930s."

I say, "I remember asking Joseph that question when I visited him in Belgium while in college and he answered the same way. Is there any more to it than that?"

I add, "Falkowski? That's not French. He always said he was born in Liege, Belgium, lived in France."

"Well, honey, it's a complicated story. Your father was born in Poland, of Jewish parents, went to Jewish schools. Falkowski was his given name." I remember briefly asking Mom if Dad was Jewish right after he died, but it didn't come up again until now.

◆ ◆ ◆

I have so many questions. How many brothers and sisters did Dad have? Did they survive the war and Holocaust? What happened to Dad's parents? Nothing comes out of my mouth. I'm transfixed by the album. She turns the page. Six eyes zero in on a picture of six people, a close-up. "This is your dad's mother, father, sister, and two brothers. Your dad is in the front, twelve years old. He was the youngest of five children, much younger than all his siblings. His name was Ilja. He changed it to Elliott after he came to the United States so he could fit in better. He also worked diligently to be fluent in English. In the late 1930s, immigrants weren't universally welcome in this country."

I stare at this family photo. I don't think I've seen it before, but oddly it looks familiar.

"This is weird. This photo looks familiar. I wonder why," I say. I get up and go get a glass of water, pondering this. Two hours pass as we leaf through pictures of siblings, cousins, classmates in grade school and high school, Dad in New York for a residency—all labeled in his handwriting.

Growing up, we never had family pictures on the walls or in frames on dressers and tables. It's right at this moment that realization hits me. Dad talked fondly about his two brothers, Joseph, whom I met, and Kola, who lived in France. But he never showed us pictures of his other family members. How amazing—he came to this country in 1937 on the *Queen Mary*, through Ellis Island, with the clothes on his back and a suitcase; he did talk about that when we were kids. All these pictures had to have been in that suitcase. With the few possessions he was able to bring, he brought pictures of the family he loved. But I never saw these while he was living nor did Carol or David ever mention seeing pictures. Dad never mentioned them. Why?

◆ ◆ ◆

"A-ha, I know why that family photo is familiar!" I say, popping up out of my chair. I have seen it. That same photo was sitting on a dresser in the apartment of Dad's brother when I visited him and his wife. I saw it in 1968 in Liege, Belgium.

I don't remember Dad talking about other family members, except for his brother David.

"Mom, I vaguely remember Dad mentioning David. And Stacy remembers more than I do. What was that story?"

"Your dad loved and looked up to his oldest brother, David, who disappeared as turmoil mounted in Europe and innocent people were uprooted and seized," Mom says. "Your dad enlisted in the US Army, was a captain, a medical doctor on the frontlines of the European theater during World War II. While over there, he asked people, he searched as best he could for David. He never found him."

All these secrets Dad kept and never told his kids. He did tell some stories to Stacy and her brother. Stacy says she remembers, when she was around nine years old, Dad talked about his family members and mentioned David. He also said some of his family were killed in the midst of the war.

The evening didn't end on that heavy note. On the last few pages of the album were pictures of Dad in his white shirt and pants, his medical work clothes, with a woman. Not Mom.

"This is Carmelita," Mom says, "your dad's girlfriend before I was in the picture. He was a charmer, the French doctor who had such a wonderful accent." Mom starts to giggle and it gains in intensity. Stacy and I can't help but join in. Our eyes start to water and I jump up to get each of us a tissue.

Lying in bed, I continue to go over those pictures in my mind. I'm discovering part of my family I never knew I had. I'm glad Mom suggested we look at the loose pictures in the box at another time. It would have been too much. Most of the pictures in the box were Dad's that he took during the war. Another day. Another day when we are ready to see and learn more.

My mind races. I learned so many new aspects of Dad's family. David was missing and Dad never found him. Dad had a larger family than I knew, some who likely didn't survive World War II and the Holocaust. Dad may have felt guilty leaving his family when he emigrated to the United States. He had so much to overcome, horror and grief, and he showed courage and determination to leave all he knew to start a new life in a new country. We had a light moment seeing his girlfriend. All this discovery fills me with empathy and admiration for Dad.

On this day new information revealed the level of trauma and heaviness Dad must have carried around all those years. It's making me realize how important it is to not hold in and carry secrets around. Might the secrets and trauma Dad carried have contributed to his heart problems? Might hiding my MS issues for so many years have made my condition worse than it needed to be?

— CHAPTER 54 —

It's Been Thirteen Years

As I think about Dad letting go of his past and embarking on a fresh start, I think about the letting go I know I have to do. I've been seeing Nancy for thirteen years now and feel like I can start flying on my own. But how will she take the news?

The next week in Nancy's office, I tell her about all the interesting information I learned about Dad from photos and stories Mom shared with Stacy and me.

"Amazing, Arlene!" Nancy says. "What an accomplishment! Your personal energy continues to open up; your family energy is opening up. You're so much more open than when I first met you. You have blossomed. In fact, I feel your openness, your Qi, and your students' Qi when you're at Heartwood teaching Tai Chi class. I love it!"

"Thanks, Nancy. I feel like I'm living what it means to take your body with you. Your words. Your advice. I'll always remember how pivotal these words have been for my healing."

"You came in so excited. As I feel your pulses, though, you seem a little on edge. What's going on?" Nancy asks.

"I am a little fidgety today." I feel my forehead is warm as I scoot around in my chair facing Nancy. I try to be my normal self, but Nancy, being so perceptive, picks up my vibe. My confidence has built up. I know how to manage my health. I've now integrated everything she's taught me. Nancy has been my support and cheerleader for my body and it's time for me to be my own cheerleader. Nancy has been a wise voice in a lot of my decision-making and now it's time to see if I can tap into my own wisdom and trust it.

"I want to ask you something," I say. A weird silence follows.

"Yes, go ahead," she says.

"I've been thinking . . . I want to ask you . . . should I think about flying on my own? I love our work together and am so motivated by your reassurance, but I don't want to be totally dependent on you for my continued healing. Oh, Nancy, I'm not sure I should have brought this up," I say, looking down at my lap. *My words are garbled. I'm not making sense. I'm so nervous.*

"It's fine, Arlene, actually good you're thinking about this. You are doing the work. You are totally committed to Tai Chi, which reinforces everything we do in this room. And don't think you're hanging on, looking to me for your health. I'm a vessel, a guide, an acupuncturist who is helping to open your energy channels and keep your Qi flowing freely."

"So, now what? I brought this up and am not sure what I want to do, if anything," I say.

"What if we schedule our appointments once a month, rather than every two weeks?" Nancy suggests.

"Okay." I'm quickly trying to think this through. It's hard to imagine not seeing Nancy. She's my lifeline to a healthy body and mind.

Will I regress, revert to old patterns without her? I jumped off a cliff when I first started to see her. Now I'm afraid I might fall off the cliff without her. But we're not talking about cutting my treatments, just meeting less often.

Just thinking about *letting go* is hard.

CHAPTER 55

A Safe Place to Be

After that conversation with Nancy, I begin seeing her once a month. Two years later, Nancy and I continue with our monthly appointments. My Tai Chi classes are going strong. Currently in my eleventh year of teaching, I have forty-eight dedicated students spread across four classes. I also teach two classes of high school kids, as part of their regular curriculum, twice a week. Often skeptical at first, the high schoolers make discoveries about themselves. "My balance is so bad," one surprised sophomore boy says, who had seemed blasé about having to take Tai Chi. He adds, "I really need this and it's already helping my soccer game."

My name is now associated with Tai Chi. I don't know why I'm still occasionally surprised when a prospective student says I've been recommended as the teacher to study with. Potential students tell me, "I want to take classes with you" or "My doctor recommended you."

Tai Chi has opened me up to a new world of energy. Not only do I have more energy, but I also have more clarity of thinking. I hear an awakening in many of my students. This is a 180-degree shift from my corporate days. The first thing I now sense about another person is their energy: positive, negative, anxious, low, calm. Energy is palpable and says a lot about where a person is.

♦ ♦ ♦

After fifteen years of working with Nancy in her treatment room, I feel confident it's time to end our regular appointments. There's no incident or specific reason that pushes me to this point. I just know. She agrees with me that it's time for me to use all I've learned to go it on my own. It reminds me of going off to college.

The air feels calm in Nancy's room as we begin our final scheduled treatment.

"Your Qi is moving freely, Arlene. Your body is strong. I mention your story to other patients because your dedication to our work and to Tai Chi has been unwavering."

"Thanks, Nancy. You've inspired and guided me to a place I didn't know was possible. Remembering how deflated I felt when my neurologist told me there was nothing more he could do for me, I couldn't have dreamed that it would be a springboard for trying a new approach, which turned out to transform my life."

As usual, Nancy offers a wise word for my upcoming transition time. "You will teach by your own example. Your story will speak louder to your students than you can imagine. You will continue to inspire. Continue to be yourself and be open. I know you will."

"Nancy, I can't thank you enough. You guided me to Tai Chi. You didn't flinch when you told me I had to take my body with me. I am so grateful."

I feel uplifted, ready to move forward into a new phase of learning and giving some wise words to others as Nancy has given to me.

♦ ♦ ♦

During the first few months, it feels weird. My body longs to be in Nancy's treatment room as she reassures and cheers for me. To give up such an affirming, life-enhancing process makes me uneasy, like giving up the training wheels on a bicycle. I am fortunate, though, that it is not a complete cutoff. Nancy continues to be the executive director of Heartwood, so I see her in the hallway or kitchen. She frequently tells me she can feel the positive Qi from my Tai Chi students flowing out of the classroom.

♦ ♦ ♦

In my classroom, I start with the familiar, "Feet and legs hip-width apart. Knees soft. Be aware of your tan t'ien, the major energy center of your body." Standing in my wide-legged black pants, red T-shirt with a yin-yang symbol on the front, I look at my students. They look unremarkable standing there, but I am fully aware of their struggles inside—pain from arthritis or fibromyalgia, anxiety and stress, lupus, spinal stenosis, high blood pressure, and more. We embrace the silent movement.

"You're so patient," they say. "This is the one place I don't feel competition, even with myself." "I feel safe here." "You listen." "You are gentle." I hear their affirmations. It's humbling. I'm a catalyst to help students get in touch with their energy, help them move it in positive ways. They are doing the work. They are uncovering and unleashing energy that is just waiting to come forward to soften, calm, and potentially heal.

I remember my first Tai Chi teacher saying we want to return to the source, the original breath, the essence of life. I remind my students that we're involved in a process to shed the shoulds, musts, and self-criticism and accept ourselves where we are.

I end the class where we began, in stillness, at our center point, feet planted, moving in slow, small circles. I read from the *Tao Te Ching*, a portion of number Sixteen:

> *Empty yourself of everything.*
>
> *Let the mind become still.*
>
> *The ten thousand things rise and fall while*
>
> *the Self watches their return.*
>
> *They grow and flourish and then return to the source.*
>
> *Returning to the source is stillness, which is the way of nature.*[2]

Those ten thousand things are the life events we experience and move through. I've been learning to pay attention, listen to my body, and muster up the courage to say it's time to try it on my own.

For so long, I thought I wasn't ready, and Nancy had to reinforce that I was. But this time, I knew that I was ready. Now I'm flying solo and it's a smooth ride.

---

2   Lao Tzu, translated by Gia-Fu Feng and Jane English (New York: Vintage Books, 1989).

— CHAPTER 56 —

"Tai Chi's Holy Place"

On a gray, dreary morning in the fall of 2010, I delve into my emails. I stop as one header jumps out at me: Tai Chi Study Trip to China. It's from Troyce, my teacher who led the workshop in Bend. I read the email and learn that she's leading a trip to China, including Tai Chi study in Chen Village and in the Wudang Mountains. My heart races. *Is this my chance, my dream come true? Is my body strong enough? Do I have the stamina to go on such a big trip?*

I've had a push-pull reaction to thinking about China for years. I long to go. I've looked over various China tours, ten days, fourteen days, all touring trips with lots of air and bus travel within the country and no Tai Chi. All the schedules looked like go, go, go from early morning until evening. This feels different. It's a specially designed trip with a focus on studying Tai Chi with masters in China. It starts in eight months. I have some time to think about this. And I don't want to overthink it. I know how to listen to my body and pay attention to my energy. Right now, I feel the energy coming out of Troyce's announcement; plus I love her teaching and her caring spirit. This is exciting.

I call Troyce to ask her if she thinks I can do it. She knows that I need to manage my energy and often rest in the middle of the day.

"Arlene, this isn't a trip where we'll get on a bus at 6:30 a.m. and tour until 6:30 p.m. Some days we'll start with joining local Chinese playing, as they call practicing, Tai Chi in a park. You'll have choices about what you want to do. I hope you'll consider it."

My mind is totally preoccupied with this possibility. Although I try not to obsess or overanalyze, I do. I make a chart of pluses and minuses. I discuss it with Mom, with my friends.

Jacque, my close college friend from Brooklyn, mentions she might be interested. It would give me a comfort to have my friend with me, to help advise me about ways to rest to avoid fatigue. I say yes and Jacque says yes. On May 4, 2011, we head to China. Fourteen of us, plus our leaders Troyce and her colleague, a retired professor from Chico University, who organized the details of the trip.

♦ ♦ ♦

A waft of cold air sweeps down across my shoulders. Shivers. I grab my black sweater that I stuffed between me and the chair armrest.

"Ladies and gentlemen, we're at cruising altitude," the captain announces. Wow, it's happening! I'm on my way to China, my dream for many years, thinking it wasn't possible. But it is possible. I never would have thought when I was laid out on my couch for two years that I'd be able to make a fifteen-hour trip to China, the source of Tai Chi, Qigong, and Taoism, and stay there for a month.

◆ ◆ ◆

Our first morning in Beijing, we enter a festive atmosphere in the Temple of Heaven Park. Everywhere I look, people are doing Tai Chi. Some are by themselves; others are in groups. It's a dream come true. So much activity, so many people, moving in unison, in silence.

We quietly move into the back of a group of women who are smiling, relaxed, enjoying moments of Tai Chi. They don't miss a beat, even though it's obvious that we're not locals. I feel welcome in the silence. It's not only peaceful but happy, light as well. I feel joy in this energy, in this moment. *I wonder if I might have lived here in a former life? It's not just comfortable; it also feels like I've come home.*

◆ ◆ ◆

Three days later, we travel by bus out of Beijing and into a countryside where the roads narrow and become bumpy gravel paths. Tiny houses line the streets. Some look like shacks that are in disrepair, dilapidated. Local Chinese men, women, and children stand and sit outside. It's in the eighties, humid, and there's no way these people enjoy any house air-conditioning. So many people everywhere, walking or riding bicycles and mopeds. Although a far cry from the twenty million living in Beijing, it seems even here people are crowded together.

We're headed to our first Tai Chi study. I start to feel anxious and intimidated about learning from a renowned Tai Chi master. Most of my fellow travelers are very accomplished teachers and graceful in their Tai Chi movements. Although I've gained so much ground in my stability and strength, I still experience occasional balance issues and my movements can be stilted when I start to fatigue. *Will I stick out in the group? Will I be able to keep up with the class?*

We approach a red building with a sign across the main entrance, *Chen Bing TaiJi Academy*. We've arrived. This is what we signed up for. Jacque and I have a sparse dorm room, with two beds and very thin mattresses, maybe about two inches thick. No pillows. We're surprised to find that we have our own bathroom with a shower on the wall. However, the shower is in the open and, when used, sprays water all over the little room! It's very rural here—gravel roads, sheep wandering about, very few cars.

We're in Chenjiago, Chen Village, in central China. Talk about source—this is the home and origin of Chen Tai Chi, the first family of Tai Chi in the modern era, birthed in the 1600s by Chen Lanting. His lineage and his energy fill this town. His statue is prominent near the entrance to the very large exhibition and museum dedicated to Tai Chi. As we walk on the narrow road to the museum, we encounter a gold rock on the side of the road with this inscription in Chinese: *Chen Village, Tai Chi's Holy Place*. I stand in silence, staring at this rock. I'm in awe of the reverence for Tai Chi and how timeless it is. It has brought me health and I owe part of that to the ancient masters who lived here, who understood the natural power of energy that they observed in nature. I feel connected to them.

Moving on from this rock, we enter a huge gate that opens to the Museum of Tai Chi. We pass a light jade split rock. The inscription on the rock says, "Everything divides into yin and yang." My mind flashes back. I've heard the words *yin* and *yang* for years, not realizing the depth of meaning that they contain. With Tai Chi, I've learned yin and yang describe the essence of life, creating balance of two opposite yet complementary energy forces. The principles and moves in Tai Chi are designed to work toward balance in all things. Starting with expanding and contracting an invisible energy ball years ago, I moved from a place of pain and uncertainty about my ability to walk to a place of confidence, knowing I can walk. Yin and yang in Chen Village brings me full circle to connect with the teachers before me who made it possible to be where I am. In silence, I utter to myself, *Thank you.* I'm grateful for Tai Chi, for it is what made it possible for me to come here.

◆ ◆ ◆

Everything around us is Tai Chi. We learn that 95 percent of the local population know and practice Tai Chi. We're walking through and being fed, not only by history but also by the very essence of Tai Chi.

The next morning, it's raining, so we start our Tai Chi practice inside, in a room a little longer and narrower than a basketball court. Floors are cement and mirrors line the walls. In my black shirt and pants, I line up with others in my traveling group, along with fifty to sixty Chen Bing Academy students. Most are young, maybe in their twenties. The Chinese teacher starts the class and is easy to follow. The language difference isn't a barrier. We are many but one in our focus on Tai Chi, which supersedes language. How wonderful it is to move together, in sync, without need for a common language.

About fifteen minutes into the class, Master Chen Bing walks in, slowly, silently among us. Wearing a long, black shirt with Chinese toggle closures and full-legged pants, he is taller than most and very handsome. He motions to us, one at a time, to go toward the far end of the room. We are ready to follow his instruction. Chen Bing is the twelfth-generation lineage holder of Chen Taijiquan and is a direct descendant of Chen Wantang. His voice is low and soft. He speaks in English and his "one" sounds like *onennnn*. "Two" is also drawn out, *twooooo*. Drawn out to help us go slower, I think. We face him and the mirrors as he leads us through silk reeling, a foundation for Chen-style Tai Chi. He tells us that Tai Chi is like silk being reeled out of a cocoon, continuous, circular, always in motion.

His calm seeps inside me. He's like a swan gliding across the still water. I feel like a swan too. At this moment I don't judge myself, wonder if I'm doing the move right. I'm in the flow of his energy, like floating across the surface of a lake, barely making a ripple in the water.

After four days with Master Chen Bing, I feel buoyed, fulfilled. If I were to go home now, I'd be satisfied. I don't have any notes or handouts to take with me. That's fine with me. I have a knowing of Tai Chi, by an international Tai Chi master in the Holy Place of Tai Chi. This experience will live with me always.

— CHAPTER 57 —

Return to the Source

Feeling so relaxed and satisfied with our four-day experience with Master Chen Bing, we change pace to touring: a bus to Luoyang, Shaolin Temple; a bullet train to Xian to see the terra cotta soldiers; a bus back to the Wudang Mountains. Antiquity mixes with modernity everywhere we go. We see so much construction of apartments and entire new towns. Steel cranes are the most consistent part of the landscape.

We arrive at Wudangshan, Hubei Province, and stop at the stone gate that will propel us into antiquity again, the Wudang Mountains. We're told this area is older than Chen Village, the place where Taoism and Tai Chi are believed to have started. I'm looking forward to a serene and peaceful experience. Since learning through Tai Chi about returning to the original source of energy, I've dreamed of visiting these mountains where it all began.

It's hot and very humid as we board our government-run bus, the only option to ascend the mountain in a vehicle. We're told it will take about fifty minutes to arrive at our hotel on the mountain. We cram into the bus with twenty other travelers, scrunched together among the luggage. Off we go on a winding road with sharp curves. The bus driver speeds up. I can't look out the window because we're on top of steep cliffs. That scares me because there's no guardrail. We reach a turn so narrow that the road is only one lane. The bus stops and honks a warning to any vehicle coming toward us. We round the curve and another and another. We hit a plateau, a flat section of pavement. Any trace of calm Qi I gained from Chen Bing is now gone.

"Everybody, off the bus," our guide tells us after the uniformed Chinese man gives him that instruction. We stand and wait and wait. We have to board another bus, a green one. To get to it, we drag our luggage up two flights of stairs and through a transportation terminal, the Wudang Transit Bus Company. I'm the envy of our group. I brought one black piece of luggage that can fit in the overhead compartment of a plane. I thought there would be a good chance we would have to carry our own luggage. I was right.

The driver of the green bus drives fast around and up the mountain that has no guardrails. I am by a window and take a quick look out. My stomach churns. This is not my image of peaceful, picturesque Wudang Mountains that I hoped to experience. *Is this worth it? Is this going to get better soon?* Fifty minutes in this speedy bus on these hairpin turns is starting to feel interminable. I'm stuck here, so I close my eyes and hope for the best.

After a half hour, we finally end the harrowing ride as we arrive at our hotel. We have to carry our own luggage up a flight of steps to get into the lobby. It is in some disrepair, so Bill, the tour organizer, goes to see a couple of rooms. He says they're not satisfactory, so we carry our luggage down the front steps into the bus again. Two people in our group whine, and not surprisingly, because they have the biggest suitcases.

◆ ◆ ◆

The next morning we're off to ascend the mountain farther. We need to ride a tram to the top. At the tram terminal entrance, there's a huge painting of Lao Tzu. He is believed to be the author of the *Tao Te Ching* and is cloaked in legend. He is followed by Taoists and has influenced Chinese thinking for many centuries. I loved learning about him in San Diego in my courses on Taoist philosophy and history.

We head up the mountain in the tram toward the Golden Summit Temple, built six hundred years ago by more than three hundred thousand workers. No rocks or trees were moved in the course of building the steps and palaces. I wonder how all those workers got up the mountain, with no roads or paths. The stones steps and monasteries were built with Taoist influence, mirroring and living in balance with nature.

"Look ahead, look up there," one of my fellow Tai Chi travelers exclaims. Coming into our view is an ancient red building, a working monastery built on the side of the mountain. Laundry on a clothes-line in the back sways in the breeze. It hits me that my experience mirrors the building of this monastery. I've had to forge my own path and climb my own mountain to create my own pillar of health.

As we exit the tram on a level rock surface, it's far from serene. Hundreds of people block any possible view of the mountain, climbing steep, winding stone steps leading to the pinnacle where the Golden Summit Temple sits. I decide to sit and rest rather than climb those uneven steps. The only free seat I find is a little stone bench, close to a small food stand. A man with a walking stick, sitting next to me, is eating a very long, peeled cucumber. A middle-aged woman with a big straw hat walks in front of me eating corn on the cob. Voices around me are loud and distracting. I close my eyes and take two deep breaths of mountain air. I try my best to visualize and feel stillness in this place of Tai Chi's birth. I can't feel or muster up a second of stillness.

◆ ◆ ◆

I'm surrounded by a swarm of tourists, noisy, more interested in snapping photos of mountains, temples, and people than experiencing them firsthand. *This isn't what I want, what I expected. This could be Dollywood. I'm so disappointed.* There's no way to be in the moment with all the foot traffic, loud talking, busy food stands. Any essence, Qi of the mountains, or footprint of Lao Tzu and his followers escapes me.

◆ ◆ ◆

After an hour and a half, our group leaves this mountain. In the afternoon we venture to the Purple Mountain Temple, in a different section of the Wudang Mountains. The eight-hundred-year-old, wooden temple houses a Taoist school with classes in session. Students and teachers are silent other than in classes. A separate nunnery is in the rear of the complex. Two large sculptures of cranes stand on their long legs in the stone foyer in front of the ancient stone steps leading up to the temple. The crane is important in Chinese culture—it represents status and longevity.

It's hot, in the upper eighties and very humid. The heat fades in comparison to what I'm encountering. It's peaceful. Silent. Reverent. This is what I thought a temple in the Wudang Mountains would look like, feel like. Embraced by silence, we climb the steep, stone steps. I'm transported back centuries. It looks and feels so old and I imagine the old sages here imparting wisdom to their students.

Women wear blue cotton jackets, a little below hip length, black pants, and black cloth shoes. Men wear deep blue knee-length jackets with white socks to the knees. Each wears Kung Fu cloth shoes with slits on the side. All men pull their long, black hair up into a knot on the top of their heads. In accordance with nature and the natural flow of the universe, they do not cut their hair.

All Taoist students practice Tai Chi every day. They get up at 4:00 a.m., run up and down those steep stone steps in front of the temple, and practice Wudang Tai Chi, movements created six hundred years ago and still practiced to this day.

I'm in the midst of a different era, set in an ancient temple with a story about to unfold. It's a throwback in time—simple living with respect and reverence for every living thing. The people grow their own food, practice Tai Chi daily, and keep their bodies strong through vigorous exercise. I love this feeling. It's what I try to capture when I do Tai Chi. It's what has helped me strengthen my body and change my perspective about what's important, changed it from a focus on achievement to being and living in accord with nature.

This is what I've longed to experience: the history, the footprints of original Tai Chi, the pristine air, and pure energy of the mountains. The peace. *This* is a moment to cherish.

— CHAPTER 58 —

Root like a Tree

The next day, we're moving through a Wudang Tai Chi form outside on the expansive stone terrace of our hotel, large enough to easily handle all sixteen of us, plus two instructors. The calm experience in the Purple Temple yesterday lingers. We begin our Tai Chi with the reminder to empty our minds, come to stillness. In my own head I see myself as one of the ten thousand things rising, and I'm observing, paying attention as we listen to our teacher. In the vast realm of all things in existence, the ten thousand things, I marvel that I'm one of those things here in China.

This Tai Chi school is under the leadership of Zhong Xuechao (Master Bing). He is out of town, so his colleague, Master Huang, teaches us, and his apprentice Derek provides translation. We shift our weight following his instruction as we learn the moves of the Wudang Five Animal Qigong form.

Although this is a different Tai Chi style from that of Master Chen Bing, the principles and centeredness are the same. We're covering many moves in a short time. I can't remember all of them. I shift to my Tai Chi state of mind to tell myself, *It's okay. Just go with the flow, listen and move your body as best you can, and all will be well.* Once I shift my thinking away from *getting it*, I relax and let go.

I look down at my black shoes with red Tai Chi letters on the side. Although I packed lightly, I made sure these shoes would be with me when practicing Tai Chi on the very soil and rocks of the mountains where Chen WangTing and Zhang Sanfeng stood, connecting my energy to the earth and to the masters in China. I feel that connection with the beginnings and centuries of Tai Chi. Standing still, I root my feet like a tree to feel the ancient roots of Tai Chi, right beneath my feet.

◆ ◆ ◆

Being in the presence of Master Huang, as with Chen Bing in Chen Village—moving slowly, centering, balancing—transports me totally into the present moment. The moves of the turtle connect to the water element, to the kidney organ system. Shifting weight gently, back and forth, stepping to the diagonal, we are one energy center, a unified breath, living the essence. Time stops.

It's my Tai Chi experiences the last few days that will forever leave an energetic and spiritual imprint in my body and psyche. The lessons I've learned haven't been in words spoken, but in creating increased awareness of my own energy movement. I am energy and that energy is timeless. Tai Chi supersedes language and cultural differences. Showing up, reaching out of my comfort zone to take this trip, is a key to more fulfillment. Some of life's revealing lessons come in silence, in listening to the spaces in between my thoughts.

After forty-five minutes, I stop, sit on a stone ledge behind the group. I'm listening to my body, which says, *Enough movement for now.* I continue my connection with the group while I sit, watching, letting my mind focus my energy as though I'm standing with the group, still one with them.

I know in the days to come we'll do more touring and see the Karst Mountains in southern China, as well as the sights of Shanghai. But for now, my energy connects with this ancient mountain.

— CHAPTER 59 —

A Beginner's Mind

I return to Chicago and take a couple of weeks off from teaching, to deal with jet lag and adjust to the change of pace of my life in Chicago. When the time comes, I'm excited to return to class.

"You're beaming, with such a sense of calm. I feel it," one of my students says as we gather for class. *I do feel a lightness of spirit. Feeling so energized by experiencing Tai Chi in China with like-minded people humbles me.*

"Thanks," I respond, feeling good in the black cotton Tai Chi pants I bought in Chen Village. "Studying with the masters and practicing in the parks really allowed the history of it all to sink in."

I tell them I'll introduce a silk reeling exercise, a basic to Tai Chi, which is like silk being spun out of a cocoon, continuous and smooth. I mention that what the masters emphasized is what my teachers and I emphasize, the principles of relaxation, alignment, rooting, and moving the body as a single unit.

◆ ◆ ◆

We're ready to start moving. To get all of us into the moment and focus on our bodies, I say to stand with feet parallel, hip-width apart, and focus on the tan t'ien. We imagine a string gently pulling us up from the top center of our heads. We shift our weight forward to the balls of our feet, back to center, on the outside of the feet, then instep and back to center. We all slowly shift our weight in a circle or side to side, visualizing our legs and feet like the trunk of a tree, rooted deeply into the earth.

A few minutes later we shift our weight in our familiar form. Crane spreads its wings . . . brush knee . . . knee strike . . . turtle steps to the corner. We're balancing yin and yang in our bodies as we move through Grandmaster Cheng Man-ch'ing's Yang Style Short Form. I'm remembering and visualizing the inspiration behind the moves; the things in China that reinforced the stillness within that Tai Chi creates; the elegant cranes in front of the Purple Temple; the calm, centering energy of the Taoist monastery; the reverence and practice of silence I saw in the students meditating as they walked within the Purple Temple.

◆ ◆ ◆

Toward the end of class one of my students asks how much longer it will be until she's no longer a beginner.

I'm immediately transported back to Chen Village and tell them a story about walking on a gravel road leading to the History Museum of Tai Chi. I recall for them the rock with Chinese writing imprinted on it: Tai Chi's Holy Place. Near the rock and museum entrance we stopped to gaze at a statue of Chen WangTing. Walking farther along a stone walkway, we approached the first of three gigantic stone gates. The outermost gate signified the earliest experience of Tai Chi, the second for those who have advanced further, and the third for those who are even more advanced. Chen WangTing told his students he was outside of the first gate. My fellow Tai Chi travelers and I looked at one another in amazement. We knew that put us way, way, way outside the first gate.

This is a great lesson, to always have the mind of a beginner, eager to learn, eager to try, eager to experience Tai Chi as if for the first time.

◆ ◆ ◆

Sixteen years ago, I jumped off a cliff into the unknown. After initially resisting, I finally let go. I'm so glad that I took those first actions to get off the couch and traverse the steps to Nancy's. I arrived at and opened up my own stone gates, of sorts. My beginner's mind has led to the most profound changes—not focusing on goals and outcomes. I shifted from living in the corporate hustle to learning how to manage and conserve my energy. I addressed my fears instead of keeping them secret. I conquered a two-inch cement curb despite the difficulty, bringing my body with me, listening to the wisdom it offers. Taking one step at a time, moving forward into the unknown, starting with that call to Nancy, one step led to another, then another. I learned that thinking about taking a step wasn't enough. The key was doing it—showing up in a new place with all my fears and doubts in tow, because of the possibility that something positive was out there, not yet imagined.

Epilogue

It's been fifty-one years since that day in Minneapolis when I was twenty-two and lost all feeling in my body from my waist down. My health continues to be excellent. In fact, I'm stronger and more stable now than I was in my twenties and thirties. I can step up on a curb and walk up a flight of stairs easily without concern that I might not make it. It took years to move through debilitating fatigue, wobbly legs, fear of falling, and feeling as if my arms and legs were plugged into an electric socket. But over time, I slowly gained balance, stamina, and strength. Now people are amazed by my story and ask me if my MS is in remission or gone. I respond that I'm not sure; I keep going forward and doing my Tai Chi, which continues to sustain and nourish me.

Tai Chi reminds me to be in the moment and focus my mind on what I'm doing right now. If it's climbing steps, that's all I'm thinking about, not ruminating about what came before or what will come after. Since teaching my first Tai Chi class in 1999, I've been like the silk being spun out of a cocoon, continuous, flowing, gaining stability and strength in my body. Although I'm likely not as graceful as others might be, I learned early on that it's okay. Tai Chi energy isn't about stiffness of limbs or movement. It's about the fluidity of energy and spirit. I've been teaching Tai Chi for twenty-one years on a regular schedule. I'm grateful to be able to teach and pass on the principles and moves of Tai Chi that have been so helpful to me. It's humbling to sit on the shoulders of great teachers, whose wisdom I continue to embrace. I think of Nancy telling me years ago that she was not the source of my healing, but a vessel through which her energy connected with mine to promote healing. Now I understand. I'm a vessel through which my teaching and energy flow.

Nancy was the catalyst to changing my life forever, for giving me encouragement and tools. It wasn't smooth sailing early. I questioned if it was working, felt intense pain some days, and at times didn't want to return. But I did. Her guidance to listen to my body took a while to understand, but once I did, my daily life began to change. I switched from trusting my mind to paying attention to my physical being. It took time because living from my neck up for so long had served me well. Until it didn't. It was my body that stopped me cold. Nancy cared about me, reassured me when it was hard. I still hear her saying it takes time when your body works to heal itself. Progress may be slow. But for every tiny step forward, she noticed and applauded me. She was always gentle but firm in her approach to continue to work on opening my energy channels. There's no magic pill, she would say.

Nancy lived out of state for awhile. She has returned to manage the Heartwood Center and we see each other in the hallways and in community meetings. I love her energy and always feel her genuine care and support for me.

◆ ◆ ◆

Throughout my work with Nancy, Mom supported me and was always eager to hear me recap my working sessions with Nancy. Mom, along with Nancy, was instrumental in my healing and finding true purpose. She offered great advice during our phone calls and inspired me to get moving when walking didn't come easily. Through our phone conversations, she motivated me to get off my couch. After one of those conversations, I hung up the phone and immediately got up, walked to my elevator to go down eleven floors, just to try to walk outside. She suggested achievable steps, to take the elevator, come back when I needed to. She applauded me for trying, for doing what I could do, and often reminded me not to focus on what I couldn't do. That advice was so important to my mental well-being and I follow it to this day. Mom was so influential in my becoming who I am. She helped shape me through her strength, perseverance, kindness, love, caring, and support, rarely drawing attention to herself. She lived her life well. She was a great mom to her three children. And such a great partner for Dad, patient and knowing how to support him.

Mom died in 2012, a year after my Tai Chi experience in China. I'm so glad she lived to see me strong, in a place where I was flourishing.

I admire Dad, too. As more of his young life came to light, it made sense to me why he kept secrets about his past and family members who didn't survive the Holocaust. He set a good example for us as he worked hard, was honest, and encouraged intellectual curiosity and lifelong learning. Carol, David, Stacy, and I have continued to research and discover more about his past. We uncovered that his brother David, whom Dad looked for when he was in Europe on the frontlines, was on a martyred physicians record from the Holocaust. It put pieces of the puzzle together of why he kept secrets, knowing the pain he had dealt with, never knowing that his brother had died.

Dad would be very happy to know that I traveled to Lodz, Poland, four years ago to see his birthplace and form a bridge with his heritage. I also connected with a granddaughter of his brother Joseph. Three years ago, I unexpectedly received an email asking if I was the daughter of Helen Van Meter, Mom's maiden name, and Elliott Faulk. It was signed by Helen G, whom I instantly recognized was a cousin on Dad's side. I was as excited as a kid on Christmas, getting the bicycle she always wanted. It turns out that she was two and I was eleven when our families had last seen each other. We now communicate regularly, and two years ago, I reunited with her in Switzerland, where she lives. How exciting it was to reconnect after sixty years! Since I don't have many cousins, it was wonderful to meet extended family. We spent hours looking at pictures of Dad, his brother Joseph, who was Helen's grandfather, and other family members.

♦ ♦ ♦

I was so happy to meet more of my father's family and I'm also grateful that I had another father figure in my life, Dr. Davies. He was the foundation of my faith. His patience, listening to my doubts about believing in any faith tradition, and answering my questions, was constant. He never judged me and was kind and reassuring at a time when I experienced so much uncertainty about my health. He comforted me after Dad died. Through his guidance, wise counsel, and preaching on Sundays, I grew to believe that God was real, loved me, and would walk with me through any trial that life might throw at me. He always provided practical advice and reinforced my determination to keep going. I wish he were still around so I could tell him about my unexpected road to regain health.

Another person who believed in me from the start was Melody. The beginning of my change from achieving goals in the corporate world to living in my body began with Melody in NYC over forty years ago. I'm grateful for her carefree approach to life and wisdom about our bodies. "Your body doesn't lie," her words of caring and caution, were absolutely right. She was there for me in those days when my body faltered. She taught me that it's okay to ask for help, okay to be playful, okay to dress up for a night in SoHo and let go of my inhibitions. She helped me feel attractive, and best of all, we laughed a lot and enjoyed loads of fun.

Amy, my best friend who inspired me to contact Nancy, died too early eleven years ago. Her spirit lives with me. I'm grateful for her and her positive *pushing* me forward, saying the right thing at just the right time. Her card with "a gentle reminder" propelled me to take a big risk that definitely paid off. She cheered me on in my ups and downs with the hard work with Nancy. She visited me often during those three years I lay on my couch, would always urge me to keep at it, keep going back to work with Nancy, keep hope that my body would respond.

Peter and I, now friends for over forty years, enjoy ballet and modern dance performances together. He continues to be a great listener and advocate for my Tai Chi and writing. It's great to have him as a close friend who knew what it was like when my struggles were big. Speaking of long-term good friends, my Heavenly Seven college friends continue vital relationships. We travel together once a year and have shared with one another as our lives have unfolded. Not having to explain ourselves is a joy, and after fifty years of knowing one another, these relationships are truly a treasure.

They were with me from the start when I was in my twenties and swimming in uncertainty. Many days I wondered if my legs would take me across the street, if I could garner the strength to make it up some steps. Uncertainty promoted fear and caused me to focus on what I couldn't or might not be able to do. What I've learned is to keep moving forward, even without answers, even without knowing outcomes. I often think of the Chinese story where the student asks the teacher, "Master, what is your lesson for me today?" He replies, "Relax, nothing is under control, just go with the flow." It's one thing to hear, *Go with the flow, let go, be in the moment.* It's another to internalize these words and live them. For me, it's taken time, patience, and determination.

Walking is precious to me, something I intentionally think about every day. Every morning I say thank you for the ability to walk. Gratitude fills my being. The wooden cane I so carefully selected years ago and that aided me for over a decade stands proudly by my front door in a multicolored, porcelain, Chinese umbrella stand. It reminds me as I walk out the door not to take walking for granted. It's a gift. Mom gave me that container to encourage me to keep going. It symbolizes her love and caring.

It was beyond my imagination that my life would unfold as it has. I didn't find Nancy. I was found. I don't feel like I sought Tai Chi. It sought out me. I didn't feel ready for either but jumped in anyway. I took a risk into the unknown, and one step at a time, it's led me to a healthy life I could not have imagined.

Acknowledgments

Nancy F: You've been a cheerleader for my body and were the catalyst for me to jump into the scary unknown, discover Tai Chi, and gain renewed health. You taught me to listen to my body and showed me possibilities I couldn't see. What a gifted healer you are and I'm so grateful for you.

Peter: When I leaned on your shoulder, sometimes literally when I could barely walk, you lifted me up and made me feel OK. Your steady friendship over the years nourishes me.

Carol: Without question, I can always count on you for support and care. Thank you for being a sister who accepts me as I am.

David: I've counted on your expert medical advice to help give me direction and connect me with the best doctors. You've always come through for me as more than just a friend but as a dear and caring brother.

Stacy: Your creative mind and hand designed my logo and class flyers, adding color and bright energy to my life. Your encouragement to keep going forward with my writing and your help in researching family timelines and history have been inspiring. You bring me joy.

My Tai Chi students: You are the impetus for writing this book. You asked me to write down my experiences, the difficult and the positive. You said hearing my story inspired you to take positive action for improving your health by taking my Tai Chi class. I admire your determination and fortitude in coming to class even when it is difficult. Your courage and personal stories are remarkable.

My Tai Chi teachers: I've been honored to be your student—to learn sound principles and moves that have been passed through generations. A special thanks to all my teachers in Chicago, southern California, and China.

Kim P: I'm thankful for your years of guidance on my website and marketing. You've been so supportive and encouraging to me in writing my story.

Nancy B: Your writing salons were my first foray into a group of aspiring authors. Your wisdom, wit, and straightforward advice inspired me to keep writing and believing that I might someday publish a memoir.

Nadine: You appeared as the right person at the right time, giving me guidance with your developmental editing and coaching expertise. I've enjoyed every moment working with you—from your earliest recommendation to turn the first eleven chapters into a short prologue, to the day you said, "Your book is ready to be published and go out into the world."

Acknowledgments

Greenleaf Book Group team: My thanks to the entire team for your enthusiasm, professionalism, and guidance. To Jen Glynn for your management of the production process, Jessica Reyes and Trish Lockard for your editing expertise, and Jeffrey Curry for attention to detail in proofreading. To Tiffany Barrientos for distribution, Amanda Marquette and Sam Ofman for marketing and digital media strategy. Mimi Bark, you took in the energy and movement of my story and translated it into a stunning book cover. I love your talent of visualization. You've all made this a seamless process.

MaryBeth: Thank you for your enduring friendship and for checking on me frequently about my health and writing. I know I can count on you for anything.

My dear and faithful friends who have walked with me for decades through the ups and downs—Dena, Jacque, Darca, Betty, Kathie, Lorraine—I love you and the University of Iowa and Gamma Phi Beta that brought us together.

To everyone mentioned in this book—supporters who motivated, inspired, and comforted me, to those who presented a roadblock that spurred me on to other options, I thank you. Teachers and guides often come in unexpected places and in unexpected packages. I've learned to pay attention and be ready.

For the calm, centering energy of Tai Chi, my meditation in motion, I'm grateful. It's an honor and humbling experience to teach and share this life-enhancing practice with others.

About the Author

Arlene Faulk has had a passion for writing from a young age, beginning in the eighth grade when she wrote and published her class newsletter, *The Tattler*. She earned a BA in journalism from the University of Iowa, reporting on everything from Led Zeppelin concerts to protests of the Vietnam War. She went on to receive an MA in speech communication from the University of Kansas. Her career path developed in the business world, where she managed human resource departments in a major airline until her body stopped her. Through a zigzag trajectory, she discovered her calling with Tai Chi. She has been teaching Tai Chi for over twenty years in Chicago and Evanston, Illinois.

For more information, please visit www.arlenefaulk.com

CPSIA information can be obtained
at www.ICGtesting.com
Printed in the USA
LVHW042319210322
713998LV00004B/421